PERSONAL BEAUTY

BY

D.G. BRINTON, M.D.

AND

GEO. H. NAPHEYS, M.D.

FACSIMILE EDITION

APPLEWOOD BOOKS
BEDFORD, MASSACHUSETTS
1994

Personal Beauty was originally published by W.J. Holland under the title *Health and the Human Form* in 1869. It was copyrighted by D.G. Brinton and Geo. H. Napheys in 1869. Applewood Books would like to thank Ruth Bragg for lending her copy of *Health and the Human Form* for reproduction.

ISBN 1-55709-226-5

Thank you for purchasing an Applewood Book.
Applewood reprints America's lively classics — books from the past that are still of interest to modern readers.
For a free copy of our current catalog, write to:
Applewood Books, 18 North Road, Bedford, MA 01730.

10 9 8 7 6 5 4 3 2 1

Library of Congress Cataloging-in-Publication Data
Brinton, Daniel Garrison, 1837-1899.
    [Laws of health in relation to the human form]
    Personal beauty: the laws of health in relation to the human form / by D.G. Brinton and Geo. H. Napheys.
        p.   cm.
    First published by W.J. Holland, 1869.
    Includes bibliographical references.
    ISBN 1-55709-226-5
    1. Beauty, Personal.   2. Hygiene.   I. Napheys, George H. (George Henry), 1842-1876.   II. Title.
RA775.B75   1994
646.7–dc20   94-4705
                                                          CIP

PUBLISHER'S NOTE

WE HAVE reproduced this book as an example of an American beauty book of days gone by. It is intended as a working guide to personal beauty. The reader is strongly advised <u>not</u> to use recipes or techniques mentioned in this book, as they have not been tested for the modern home.

Time has been kinder to social attitudes than it has to personal beauty. When we look back on the olden days we are sometimes embarrassed to see racial and social stereotyping, and phrases that conjure up some response in the modern reader that was not felt by the reader of the times. These books are part of our heritage. They are a window on our real past. For that reason, except for the addition of this note, we are presenting *Personal Beauty* unedited from its first edition.

GRECIAN FEMALE.

THE

LAWS OF HEALTH

IN RELATION TO THE

HUMAN FORM.

BY

D. G. BRINTON, M.D.,

ASSISTANT EDITOR OF THE MEDICAL AND SURGICAL REPORTER, LATE SURGEON
U. S. V., AND MEDICAL DIRECTOR OF THE ELEVENTH ARMY CORPS,
MEMBER OF THE ACADEMY OF NATURAL SCIENCES OF
PHILADELPHIA, ETC.

AND

GEO. H. NAPHEYS, M.D.,

ONE OF THE EDITORS OF THE HALF-YEARLY COMPENDIUM OF MEDICAL SCIENCE,
MEMBER OF THE PHILADELPHIA COUNTY MEDICAL SOCIETY, CORRES-
PONDING MEMBER OF THE GYNÆCOLOGICAL SOCIETY OF
BOSTON, AUTHOR OF THE "COMPENDIUM OF
MODERN THERAPEUTICS," ETC. ETC.

———

" Discite quæ faciem commendat cura, puellæ,
Et quo sit forma tuenda modo."—Ovidius Naso.

———

SPRINGFIELD, MASS.:
W. J. HOLLAND.
1870.

PREFACE.

SINCE the publication, now thirty odd years ago, of the excellent little book of Dr. John Bell, we do not know of any work in this country on Personal Beauty, written from the physician's point of view. In Europe, on the other hand, the subject has occupied some of the best writers in the profession; and in view of the vast increase in cosmetic arts within the past few years, it must be regarded as one of great public and professional, as well as personal interest. We have endeavored in the present volume to furnish such an abundance of simple and harmless, yet efficient aids for the toilet, that the dependence on secret and injurious nostrums may be dispensed with, and the beauty of the body cultivated more in accordance with the principles of correct taste and sound health than is now the case.

THE AUTHORS.

155 NORTH NINTH STREET,
PHILADELPHIA, PA.

CONTENTS.

THE HAIR.

PERSONAL BEAUTY.

INTRODUCTORY.

WOMEN are now young longer than they are beautiful. This book is designed to teach them how to be beautiful longer than they are young. Is it worth while to do this? Let us look in history for a reply.

The most intellectual woman at the court of the First Consul was Madame de Staël; the most beautiful was Madame Récamier. Madame de Staël was not pretty, and her talents brought her fame rather than love. Madame Récamier, though with some claims to be a *bel esprit*, gained no distinction by her learning, but brought every one to her feet by her beauty. The two were not rivals, and therefore they were friends. Each saw the other's power, and we have it on record that Madame de Staël said more than once that she would gladly exchange her intellectual superiority for the beauty of Madame Récamier.

(9)

Does it need this anecdote to vindicate the power of personal charms, "the proud strength of beauty," as an old writer fitly expresses it? We could relate a hundred others to the same effect. There is Coleridge, the most brilliant talker of this century, who somewhere complains with comical chagrin how often, as in some ball-room he held a circle of listeners spellbound by his wondrous discourse, he had seen his hearers slip away one by one when the belle of the evening appeared. It was so in all times. Phryne, the most beautiful woman of Athens in the days of Phidias and Praxiteles, had a cause of importance to try before the court. Lest her peerless charms should deflect the scales of justice, she was ordered to appear veiled. But when she found the judges were about to pronounce against her, she threw aside her drapery, and so biased their minds by the sight of her beauty that straightway they decided in her favor.

Would Judith, think you, have saved her country and won a fame imperishable, had she not been as comely a Jewish maiden as ever crushed with white feet the purple grapes of Olivet?

This is true that the poet sings—

> "Plus oblige, et peut davantage,
> Un beau visage,
> Qu'un homme armé."

As nothing is more powerful, so few things are more noble than personal beauty. It is a shallow

fashion to decry it, to affect to hold it lightly, to pass
it by as transitory and superficial. That it is fleeting
is true, and more the pity. more the reason that we
should guard it well. and appreciate it while it lasts.
For it is this beauty, "skin-deep" if you will, that
inspired the pencil of Raphael and the chisel of
Michael Angelo. It is this which renders the works
of the great masters of art immortal, which invests
their productions with a sweet and mighty influence,
which gives them a value beyond what dollars and
cents can possibly express.

Plato, profoundest of heathen philosophers, explor-
ing this universe in search of God, whom as yet no
revelation had disclosed to the Gentile world, found
Him nowhere so manifestly present as in Beauty, and
with this as his last word the thinker returned to
earth.

Trivial philosophizers of modern times have been
unable to make anything out of this. With dry eru-
dition they would show us that this matter of personal beauty is a mere caprice of the fancy; that in
Abyssinia the ideal woman is a mass of fat, a Dulcinea
of four hundred weight or so, while in China she must
be as lank and lean as the brown sea-sand; that the
Caffirs delight in a black skin, thick lips, a flat nose,
and large flabby ears; that the Peruvians aim to
acquire a distorted head and prominent cheek bones;
and many similar diversities of taste. From all this

they draw the conclusion that there is, in fact, no absolute type of beauty, that it is solely a question of race and education.

What a lame conclusion it is!

We can show them in turn that the Fejee Islanders think it quite the proper thing to kill and eat their aged parents; that theft and murder are no crimes to the Kamschatkan, but that to scrape the snow from his shoe with a knife is a heinous sin which he will in nowise commit; that to lie and steal were not amiss in ancient Sparta, but to be found out was a punishable offence; that to destroy an infant which was not well formed was in the same state an approved custom, but to employ silver money was an infraction of the law. Does all this invalidate those eternal principles of truth, justice, goodness, and love, which lie at the base of the teachings of true religion, and the instructions of its ministers?

Not in the least.

Then, we answer, neither do those various and false notions of personal beauty in the least detract from the reality of an absolutely perfect form of personal human beauty.

But we do not stand in need of a theory to prove this. The verdict of art and the incontrovertible evidence of the most exact of sciences are at our command.

Where do the painter and the sculptor of to-day seek

their highest models? In those discolored and broken marbles chiselled nigh three thousand years ago in Greece. All that we have since learned does but teach us the more forcibly that these illustrate the eternal laws of beauty.

These laws are those of geometry.

"You don't mean to make this a treatise on the higher mathematics?"

Heaven forbid. There is no such matter in our thoughts. But we do want to say in reply to those stupid philosophizers who can see nothing absolute in the ideal of beauty, that the curves and outlines of perfect human figures can be geometrically constructed by the rule of harmonic ratio; that they can be derived from the laws of the vibration of a monochord; that they are, therefore, as much in a strait-jacket of mathematics as are the notes of a musical instrument; that all this and a great deal more to the purpose has been proven by the researches of an English writer whose name is D. R. Hay, and that—

But enough, or we shall strike the very rock we are steering to avoid, and overwhelm ourselves in a sea of technicalities. Let it only be remembered that personal beauty is a harmony of form and color quite as severely regulated by mathematical formulæ, yet capable of quite as infinite variations as that other harmony we call music.

"What is Beauty?" some one once asked Goethe.

2

"I do not know, but I can show it to you," he replied.

We shall follow the advice of this great master, and, troubling ourselves no further as to the ultimate nature of Beauty, we shall rather inquire *how it is to be got, and how it is to be kept.*

These inquiries will appear to some the most important in the world, and to others the most trivial. We do not quite agree with the former; but we are still further in opinion from the latter. Yet these will be chiefly found in our own profession. Physicians look at the human body not as a "model," but as a "subject." They measure, and probe, and dissect it, not to learn what it is in its utmost perfection, but in order to detect the more readily its degradations and abasements. Then, again, they see so much of the miseries and accidents to which it is exposed, that they think people are well enough off when they are in health, and have no business to waste time in trying to become beautiful.

The period has been when this was all very well. It is right to provide the necessaries ere we cast about for the luxuries of life. Leather and wool should precede lace and diamonds.

But apart from the fact that in a sense health and good looks are synonyms, the hour is now come when the improvement. the maintenance, if possible the creation of personal beauty, deserve to be recognized as forming a legitimate and worthy department of medicine. "Cosmetics," it should be called, if one can rid that word of its current baser meaning as applied to the meretricious arts of the toilette.

If one reflects how much mental suffering even slight deformities give, and how often the loss of beauty is the forerunner of the loss of health, it will not seem idle or unworthy of the highest medical skill to take cognizance of such trifles. Indeed, each generation witnesses more and more attention paid to

"Reparer des années les irreparable outrages,"

as the gallant and oft-quoted line of Racine phrases it.

This department of "cosmetics," "*chirurgica cosmetica*," as the old surgeons styled it, of which we speak, is a border-land between science and idealism, between the physician and the artist, and must henceforward take its position as an important field of professional industry.

It is, we say, a border-land between the physician and the artist. It is wholly within the province of neither. Health is the source of beauty, but the stream does not stay forever by its fountain. All the precepts, all the hints, which the diligent study of the healing art gives, all the suggestions proffered by hygiene and physiology, we shall attentively consider and apply. But is this all? By no means. Then come those aids to beauty provided by chemistry and pharmacy, those secret arts and mysteries of the toilette, by which we outdo nature at her best, and crown her highest efforts with an added glory.

If we take under our special charge this slighted branch of study, if we seek to bend to its elucidation whatever the austere oracles of medicine and the humbler artisans of the shops can furnish us, let not the effort be disdained. Innocent devices to heighten the effect of beauty have nothing derogatory about them. For, as the wisest of poets has said:—

> "Nature is made better by no mean,
> But nature makes that mean: so, o'er that art,
> Which, you say, adds to nature, is an art
> That nature makes.
> *　*　*　* This is an art
> Which does mend nature—change it rather: but
> The art itself is nature."

It is our intent to lay down those rules by which the most desirable form, color, and grace in the human body can be obtained and preserved; and further to tell of those artifices, if you will, by which these qualities can be imitated when they cannot be acquired. Some of these means are dangerous and injurious. Against them we shall speak words of warning. Others are harmless; and to them there can be no objection from the physician's point of view. But we know our responsibility does not cease here. Do we run the danger of ministering to vanity, or to deceitfulness?

There is no vanity, necessarily, in making the best of ourselves; and a desire to please others in our appearance, as well as in our actions, has nothing about it reprehensible. What good thing may not be applied to some ignoble end? There is nothing blameworthy in the love of beauty, nor in its cultivation; nothing contrary to purity or religious faith.

It has been well said by a genial writer, Mr. James Bruce: "All the arguments against women using every art to heighten and preserve their charms resolve themselves into the hateful belief of the ascetic, that everything that is offensive to man is agreeable to heaven, and all that is agreeable to man is offensive to God—a belief that has characterized all false religions from the beginning of time to the present hour." Did we think differently, no word of ours should be spoken in favor of personal beauty and its enhancement.

These cares and arts will enable many a wife to recover and to retain the affections of her husband, and many an unmarried woman to obtain that attention and courtesy the want of which gives her now unhappy moments.

That, as some have said, these arts encourage deceitfulness, is not to be accepted. For the same reason we should discard wigs, false curls, false teeth, and a host of other devices to conceal deformity, which are now in universal use.

What results may not flow from this self-cultivation?

What a fine thing it will be when women shall combine the comeliness of youth with the wisdom of age! It is not without precedent.

Diana of Poictiers, Duchess of Valentinois, was the reigning beauty at the courts of three successive kings of France. The historian Brantôme knew her well. "I saw this noble dame," he tells us, "when she was seventy years of age, and she was as charming, as fresh, and as lovely as any lady of thirty. Her beauty, grace, and majesty were such as she had ever possessed. 'Tis a pity that such a body is now buried in the earth. It was said that certain skilled doctors and subtle apothecaries prepared for her daily a potion of soluble gold, and that this or some similar drug it was that preserved her beauty." Soluble gold it was not, Seigneur Brantôme, but another and potent recipe, which is not yet lost.

"And this recipe is —?"

Patience! we are not yet at that part of our subject. The secret of the famous Diana of Poictiers is not to be lightly told at the beginning of a book. The prudent traveller spares his funds at the outset of his journey, and is only generous to well-tried companions. But rest assured that the Fountain of Youth yet flows for her who diligently seeks it.

And now we shall try a definition. They are notoriously difficult to make, and probably we shall have no greater success than many another.

What is personal beauty ?

It is the combination of correct proportion and color with perfect performance of function.

Perfect performance of function requires health and grace; proportion and color are under the control of fixed laws of taste.

In accordance with this definition, our plan shall be to take up the human body as a whole, and then in its several parts, and show first what is the true artistic ideal of perfect form in each. Then we shall examine one by one the defects and imperfections to which each is subject, and how these may be remedied either by medical or by cosmetic art. Many such flaws in nature's handiwork we shall find may readily be prevented, or cured, or, at least, concealed, by simple means within the reach of all. But others require the hand of the surgeon or the skill of the physician. It is gratifying to think how few blemishes there are that by one or another means at our command may not be lessened or wholly removed.

For the matter of color, which includes the complexion, etc., we shall treat of that in a chapter devoted to the skin; and as the hair is, in the language of anatomy, an appendage of the skin, what we have to say about it will find an appropriate place at the close.

That other branch of personal beauty which treats of dress, the arrangement of the hair, and the study of corporeal grace, we shall but casually touch upon, as it lies almost wholly aside from medical science, and within the exclusive jurisdiction of the artist.

But at the outset our fair reader who would be fairer must not understand us as promising too much. We do not come with an Elixir of Youth and Beauty, which she can drink at a draught, and bid defiance to Old Time? No! but in a hundred ways, here a little and there a little, by obeying rules of health, by diet and exercise, by devices of surgery, and by mysterious arts of pharmacy, she will learn how to transform herself from homely into passable, from passable into attractive, from attractive into beautiful.

Is this candid confession a disappointment?

Alas! after all, it is only by self-denial that we can gain anything of consequence in this disjointed world of ours. *Il faut souffrir pour être belle;* if we wish beauty, we must bear a smart or two. We must put up with them. There is no other way. Though many a one is like the French lady who announced her intention of visiting England, but declared she would not go by sea, as she was certain to be sea-sick.

" But, madame," objected one of her hearers, " England is an island."

"Oh yes, of course it 's an island," she replied; " I know that well enough. But then, isn't there some way, perhaps, of passing around and reaching it by land?"

THE HUMAN FIGURE AS A WHOLE.

EVERY young lady who has taken drawing lessons —and nowadays, when fashionable seminaries teach all the arts and sciences, what young lady has *not* done so?—knows that there are certain rules by which we form the outlines of the human figure. Each part must be in proportion to the others.

These rules were derived from a very careful study of the most celebrated ancient statues, and from measurements of the finest living models. They cannot be transgressed, even in the smallest degree, without offending a practised eye. The story is told of Lavater, the celebrated physiognomist, that on one occasion he visited a portrait painter to look over his productions. Presently he stopped before one of the paintings, and, pointing to the ear, declared that it was impossible that that organ, as represented, could have been associated with the other features. The artist, in surprise, confessed in that instance the sitting had been incomplete, and that he had painted the ear from memory only. Fortunately few people are so critical as Lavater, or the artists would have a sad time.

We have no intention of going into such minutiæ, only proposing to give in general terms what the human figure should be, and what we shall say applies particularly to the female figure. For men and queens, says an old French proverb, have the privilege of being ugly, *aux hommes et aux reines on passe la laideur.*

The height should be exactly equal to the distance between the tips of the middle fingers of either hand when the arms are fully extended. Ten times the length of the hand, or seven and a half times the length of the foot, or five times the diameter of the chest from one armpit to the other, should also each give the height of the whole body. The distance from the junction of the thighs to the ground should be the same as from that point to the crown of the head. The knee should be precisely midway between the same point and the bottom of the heel. The distance from the elbow to the tip of the middle finger should be the same as from the elbow to the middle line of the breast. From the top of the head to the level of the chin should be the same as from the level of the chin to that of the armpits, and from the heel to the toe.

With these measurements at command any one can readily find out how near she approaches to the perfection of form. But let her not be dismayed at discovering sundry discrepancies. The matter is not to be understood too rigidly. These rules are intended to apply to a certain age and a certain style of beauty, and though true as rules, like all rules, they permit exceptions and suffer limited variations.

HOW TO PERFECT THE FIGURE.

Who would have a perfect form cannot begin too early. Nay, the mother should commence the physical education of the child long before its birth. Thus did the dames of ancient Greece who gave the world a race unmatched for beauty in all history.

So, too, during the period of nursing the careful mother will see to it that her child has abundance of good wholesome food, for nothing so certainly produces deformity as ill-nourishment. She will take care that the infant does not lie more frequently on one side than the other, for this will make it "lopsided;" that it is changed from arm to arm in nursing and carrying for the same reason; that it does not walk too soon, lest it become bandy-legged; that it does not wear tight clothing or bandages, as these will readily press its tender flesh and yielding bones into uncouth shapes.

Another period of life, where it is of the greatest importance that sedulous and intelligent care should guard over the child, is when she is passing through that momentous change which transforms the girl into the woman.

Very much has been said of late years of the value of well-regulated gymnastic exercise as a means of health, and it were difficult to say too much on that topic. But comparatively little has been done or said with reference to increasing the beauty of the form by such means. To be sure, there is the art called "Calisthenics," from two Greek words meaning beauty and strength, but its aim has been confined to the latter quality only. So it is with gymnastics in general. Yet it must be remembered that it is very unusual in man, and still more so in woman, to find the graceful form of perfect symmetry connected with uncommon muscular vigor, or even remarkable powers of endurance. This is a familiar fact to surgeons who examine recruits for the army and the naval service.

The old Greeks, from whom we have learned so much concerning beauty, knew this very well, and divided, therefore, their gymnastic exercises into three classes. The first was for training the soldiers to severe, protracted labor, where endurance was the quality required; the second was for the athletes, the participants in the Olympic, Isthmian, and Pythian games, who sought to combine power with activity; while the third class had as ·its object the development of harmonious proportion, the correction of defects in the figure, and the cure of vices of conformation. It is this third class of gymnastic exercises which is peculiarly suitable to girls and women. all the movements being moderate, and designed to call into play each of the muscles in proportion to its prominence in the perfect human form. Such culture causes a rapid and astonishing improvement in the figure, and we hope that it will soon be introduced into all our leading seminaries, as it already has been in some.

DEFECTS IN STATURE; TOO TALL OR TOO SHORT.

American women, as a rule, measure between five feet two inches and five feet four inches in height. Those who are much above or much under these figures will be unpleasantly aware of the fact. They should remedy it. But how? Is there anything more wholly out of all range of possibility than to grow shorter or taller at will? Is it pretended that nowadays by taking thought one can add a cubit to his stature?

No! our pretensions do not extend that far. But we profess to have some hints which may be of service even here. Most persons have read more or less about Louis XIV. It is not easy to escape him in French literature. He was called by his courtiers Louis le Grand, and as it is difficult to break an old habit, the adjective clings to him still. Well, all the memoirs of his time speak of him as of commanding stature, and we might suppose from their descriptions he was at least six feet in his stockings. In fact he was about five feet seven inches, and the rest of his height was

3

made up by high heels, a judicious costume, and a perruque of magnitude. If we learn nothing else about him, it is worth while to know this, for it illustrates how readily a diminutive person can conceal this defect of nature.

It is not so easy, one might think, to veil unusual height. In sooth it is a more serious problem, though it is not wholly discouraging. Those who have visited the galleries of the Louvre in Paris will recall an ancient and celebrated statue known as the Venus of Milo. We know not whether others have had the same experience, but for ourselves we sate before that marble wonder for hours studying its perfect outlines, its matchless drapery, its depths of expression, and it never occurred to us that the height was extraordinary. Our astonishment was great on seeing in some guidebook that it measured six feet two inches. The faultless proportions prevent any impression of excessive size in this

> "Daughter of the gods, divinely tall,
> And most divinely fair."

The same is constantly observable in life. Persons whose forms correspond closely to the artistic model rarely appear either too tall or too short, and those who have from nature these defects in growth should devote unusual attention to the symmetrical development of the body by gymnastic exercise, and practise those modes of costume adapted to their size.

They should likewise bear in mind that height depends chiefly on the length of the lower limbs and not on the body, so that when sitting tall and short persons present very little difference.

WANT OF SYMMETRY OF THE BODY.

It is a curious fact to consider that our body is formed of two entities united together. One side of us has nearly all the organs that the other has, and arranged in almost precisely the same manner. What is the use of two ears, two eyes, two nostrils, when one would, and at a pinch does answer the purpose quite as well? We do not know.

Still more curious is it to observe how the one side generally gets the better of the other, and becomes stronger, handsomer, and more adroit. Even the two halves of our body, twin brothers *on ne peut pas plus*, cannot live together without rivalry. Generally it is the right half that comes out winner. This is supposed to be because the great bloodvessels, as they leave the heart, are so arranged as to carry that side more nourishment. More rarely it is the left, and only occasionally do we see a person who can control the muscles of either side with equal power. In most persons the difference between the development of the two sides is quite visible in every member.

Now if we examine the finest statues in this respect we shall find no such inequality. Indeed, one of the first objects which an able teacher of gymnastics proposes to himself is to equalize the strength and skill of the two arms and legs.

Frequently a want of symmetry is due to the bad habit of sleeping mostly on one side. We can recall quite a number of such instances. Such a habit should never be indulged. It is ruinous to grace in walking, and has, moreover, an injurious effect on the general health by displacing the internal organs, and subjecting them to unequal pressure. We always urge those whom we have the privilege of advising to sleep quite as often on the one side as on the other, and, if they can, occasionally on the back. Persons who are accustomed to sleep together should change sides from time to time. This is especially important in young girls.

Why some persons are left-handed is not clear. It is not merely a habit they learn in infancy. We have known every precaution taken with children to prevent it, tying a bag over their left hands, fastening it in the sleeve or to the side, and other devices, for months together, but without success. Nevertheless, all these means should be tried, and, when they fail, the child must be taught to use both hands alike—to be "ambidextrous," as it is called—which is rarely impossible. Left-handed people, however "dexterous" they may be, are apt to create an unpleasant sensation of awkwardness in the minds of observers. In French, *gaucherie*, from *gauche*, the left, means clownishness.

It is next to impossible for an adult to overcome this habit. The best they can hope for is to gain a sufficient command over the right arm and hand to be able to use it at table, at the blackboard, etc., as others do. Still, they have for their consolation the example of many a poor fellow in the war, who having lost his right arm has acquired singular proficiency in a year or two with his left. We have in our possession several autograph letters of that distinguished soldier and philanthropist Major General Howard, who lost his right forearm at the battle of Fair Oaks. They were written about eighteen months subsequent to his wound, and the penmanship is quite legible and. regular.

A want of symmetry in the shoulders is very common among those who write or paint steadily. The right shoulder usually becomes higher, and the bones more prominent. These persons should practise daily and regularly sitting with the left shoulder elevated and the right depressed. They should avoid low-necked dresses, and on state occasions conceal the lack of uniformity by a soft padding. A course of calisthenics is also of great service.

There is a complaint which would be comical were it not so distressing to the sufferer. It is that in which there is a partial palsy of one-half of the face. The effect is most singular. Look at one side, and it may be smiling and full of expression; look at the other and it is motionless and inexpressive. In a much less degree this effect is not unusual. Often there is a want of innervation, that is, the nerve force is not distributed equally to the two sides of the face, and one-half does not correspond exactly to the other. If we examine faces critically from in front (not from the side, as there the profile common to both halves confuses our judgment) we shall rarely find one in which the sides perfectly correspond. This is a misfortune or a fault which generally can, and always ought, to be remedied. When the difficulty is in the innervation, electricity applied by a skilful hand is of benefit; in other cases continued pressure or friction is effective.

RELAXED AND STOOPING FIGURES.

It is the proud distinction of man to walk upright. Every other animal must bend and hug the earth. Stooping we associate with age and infirmity. Therefore an erect figure has ever been deemed essential to beauty. Only some passing vagary of fashion would sanction a " Grecian bend." No one in the least acquainted with the laws of beauty would adopt or approve it.

A figure straight, lithe, and graceful will excuse a multitude of faults. It can be acquired with great certainty if proper care is taken during the period of growth.

One of the most common blemishes is that of being "round-shouldered"—stooping forward with the upper third of the spinal column. This destroys the contour of the neck and the *pose* of the head. It throws the shoulders upward and forward, entirely depriving them of their natural, graceful slope. The *chest* is also hollowed, and the swell of the breast is thereby lost. Sometimes this habit is a consequence of debility or disease. It then demands special medical treatment. For ordinary cases exercise with light dumb-bells, and a careful avoidance of continuing long in stooping positions, will suffice. Shoulder-braces are largely sold, designed to hold the shoulders back. They are of value, but only as subordinate aids. What is wanted is to strengthen the muscles of the back, and qualify them to do their duty without fatigue and without assistance.

There is a disfiguring and painful disease called curvature of the spine. Thousands of women in this country suffer the agony of the rack, are hindered from all active usefulness or pleasure, and are well-nigh deformed by this terrible complaint. It frequently arises from some imprudence in "getting up" after a confinement, sometimes from an injury, and very often from neglect of health at the epoch of change in young girls. It undermines their health

just as they are budding forth into womanhood, blast-
ing their prospects when fairest, and shrouding in
gloomy clouds the bright morning of life.

The reader may find elsewhere portrayed minutely
the insidious, stealthy advance of this disease.[1] Here
we have to do with its prevention and its cure. It
often leads to what is called "spinal irritation," and is
usually treated by blisters, by cups, by scoring the
back with hot irons, and by long continuance in bed.
These severe remedies may bring good results, but in
most cases an entirely different and milder method
may be employed with the best effect. It is that by
support. The spine, the shoulders, and the sides are
propped and sustained by light steel braces with springs
and pads, so that the curvature is impossible. The patient is quite as much at rest when standing as when in
bed, and the irritation and pain, caused as they are by
the pressure of the spine in its unnatural position, disappear at once. We have known women who had never
stood up for years, without suffering, walk erect and
with ease as soon as a carefully-made, accurately-fitting
brace was applied. But such an instrument must be

---

[1] The Physical Life of Woman: Advice to the Maiden,
Wife, and Mother. By Dr. George H. Napheys. This work
has been highly recommended by the medical press of the
country as a practical hygienic guide.

adjusted with scrupulous exactitude to fit the figure, or it will do more harm than good.

The same means may be applied with very beneficial results in another deformity quite common and indirectly quite noticeable; this is when the form is lost by child-bearing. This is often accompanied with distressing sensations of "goneness" and emptiness at the pit of the stomach. It gives a stoop to the figure and a shuffling gait. A well-fitting support here is all that is required.

One of the most common causes of ungracefulness in motion remains to be told. It lies in diseases peculiar to women. None but the physician knows how frequent these diseases are. None but he fully appreciates what a terrible foe they are to beauty, not to speak of health and happiness. The lady reclining on the *fauteuil*, and the wash-woman standing at the tub, victims to these distressing maladies, alike reveal in the positions they assume, and in the gait they adopt, an unconscious effort to "save themselves," and to avoid the suffering which an unwary motion or a painful position gives.

What a marplot this is to beauty! What chance is there for free and supple motion when pain strikes through one at every unconsidered turn! And how common is the misfortune!

It were vain for us to go at length, or at all, into this subject. We can only say that so long as such a condition exists, grace in motion is impossible, and personal beauty of all kinds is endangered. Three-fourths of those American women who grow old, fade, and wither before their time, owe their premature age to neglected or ill-treated disease of this character. Therefore they should make every effort by a careful hygiene to avoid them.

We have recently been consulted by several ladies from the Southern States for a peculiar condition of the system which they say is not unusual there, and which they attribute to the mental anxiety, the prostration of hopes, the losses, and the change in social condition, brought about by our civil war. This is a general relaxation of the muscular system. They were not emaciated, nor did they suffer any pain, or appear in bad health. But the muscles were soft and ill-defined, the gait shambling and irregular, and the motions awkward, and made with disproportionate effort of the will. They had taken quantities of the usual tonics without avail, and were almost in despair. We prescribed the daily use of electricity, medicated douche baths, warm and cold, friction, a regulated diet, and no medicine. These means, together with change of air, resulted satisfactorily in all from whom we have since heard.

Besides such general causes of relaxed and stooping figures, there are others which come strictly within the province of medicine. There are various diseases, acute and chronic, which lead to the same defects. But these will always be brought to the notice of the medical adviser, who, we hope, will bear in mind that he has before him in the case of every woman a double duty, first to save her life and health, and secondly to preserve her personal charms.

SUPERFLUOUS AND DEFECTIVE MEMBERS.

Nature, at times, plays curious freaks. Generation after generation, in some families, come into the world with six toes, or a double thumb, or a cleft lip. All who have perused Hawthorne's delightful romance, "The Marble Fawn," will remember what he says about the furry and pointed ears which from time immemorial had distinguished the Counts of Monte Beni. They took a sort of pride in the trait, but to most persons in whom such a variation from nature's plan appears, not as the certain stamp of ancient lineage, but as an annoying defect, any such peculiarity is distressing. The advice of all good surgeons is to have a superfluous member trimmed or lopped quite off in early childhood, or as soon as possible thereafter.

Occasionally, but, thank heaven, rarely, a more astonishing deformity of this nature appears. We were present at an operation some years ago where a distinguished surgeon of Philadelphia removed from the cheek of a child some months old a second and distinct child, which had been growing from that portion of the face from before birth, a sort of parasite, deriving its life from that of its twin sister.

Instances are also known of children born without an arm, or a leg, or some other member. When we were denizens of the Quartier Latin, in Paris, haunting the precincts of the École de Médecine, a woman used to stand daily on the Pont Neuf across the Seine, asking alms, and to excite the pity of the passers-by, showing her arms, each of which terminated above the elbow in a button of flesh. She had been so from birth. Probably some of our medical readers will recall her case, as Professor Paul Dubois used occasionally to exhibit her before his class.

The loss of a member by accident is much more frequent. To whatever cause the deformity may be owing, modern art offers a ready and admirable resource in the "artificial limb." Several expert mechanicians and eminent surgeons have devoted their abilities to perfecting these contrivances, until now there is little left to be desired. The limbs are faultless in form, light, easily adjusted and removed, and not very-dear. Miss Kilmansegg with her golden leg is quite behind the times, for now her gold will buy her a more shapely leg of wood and steel than ever she owned in the flesh. The spokes and fellies of the human wheel have been so thoroughly studied and closely imitated, that the most critical eye can no longer detect the presence of an artificial limb when

properly made and used. The wearer may walk, or
even waltz, with his leg of human make, and write
readily with the hand he has bought of the manufacturer.

ON CORPULENCE AND LEANNESS.

Brillat Savarin is a charming writer, and his *Physio-*
logie du Gout is a delightful book, racy and *spirituel.*
But he has now and then a naughty vein of satire.
For instance, in one passage he says it is the life-study
of every woman, at least of every pretty woman, to
become either a *little* stouter or a *little* thinner. Now
of course we reject any such aspersion as this, but
then it is true, and we don't deny it, that the precise
medium between corpulence and leanness is hard to
attain and harder to keep; so that if this matter
attracts a good deal of attention, it is nothing more
than right, æsthetically speaking, that it should. And
when such a condition of body goes on to the extent
of obesity on the one hand, or emaciation on the other,
what charms can survive the heavy change?

Look at a siren of two hundred and fifty pounds, some
female Falstaff. Her cheeks are red and swollen, her
eyes are half hidden by the folds of flesh, her voice is
short and husky, her figure is that of a barrel, her
walk is a waddle. None but an Abyssinian can take
her for a beauty. Add to this, that such a load of
flesh is a positive discomfort, and often a distress,

4

equal to a disease. The movements are slow and painful, exercise is next to impossible, many little actions cannot be performed. She cannot button her own gaiter or stoop to pick up a pin. She is unequal to going up and down stairs, to shopping on foot, to dressing her own hair. Dancing, horseback riding, calisthenics, these are out of the question. Sluggishness of body soon brings sluggishness of mind, and her slowness to follow in conversation and her inaptness in repartee add themselves to the unfavorable impression her bulk produces.

We hardly know whether the opposite condition is not quite as deplorable. Who can admire hollow eyes, prominent cheek bones, sunken cheeks, angular and shrunken shoulders where the low-necked ball-dress displays at the most inopportune season the sharp collar bones and edges of the shoulder blades, the flat breast and narrow chest, the skinny arms, the shrivelled hands, and the thin ankles? How many a once plump and blooming girl answers this description after a few years of fashionable life, and neglect of simple and easy rules of health?

If we have drawn these sketches with inexorable fidelity, it is not to give an additional sting to those already painfully conscious of their unprepossessing aspect; it is only with a view to make the careless fully aware of their defects, and to inspire them with an earnest determination to escape such a fate, whether it be already present, or only impending.

" Escape, yes, that is easily said, but how ? *Can* we escape ?"

It can be done. Physiology and medicine can now prescribe certain diets, administer certain drugs, lay down certain rules, which control so definitely the increase and decrease of flesh, that any one not a victim to actual disease can diminish or add to his weight with as much certainty as he can do the same with a domestic animal. These diets, these drugs, these rules, we shall now proceed to describe plainly and minutely, so that any one can follow them without doubt or hesitation.

And first, it is important to know what is the proper weight which a person ought to have in the eyes of the physician and the artist. This depends on several factors. It is always in proportion to the height, but is less in woman than in man, and greater in the same sex as years advance. We take as our standard a woman between twenty-five and thirty years, and give the following table of what her weight should be in proportion to her height—

If her height is 5 feet she should weigh 110 pounds.

"	"	"	5 feet 1 inch	"	115	"
"	"	"	5 feet 2 inches	"	120	"
"	"	"	5 feet 3 inches	"	125	"
"	"	"	5 feet 4 inches	"	130	"
"	"	"	5 feet 5 inches	"	135	"

and so on, adding five pounds for each additional inch of height. This scale when applied to men should be increased by from ten to twelve pounds, as the bones are larger, the muscles firmer, therefore the body for the height heavier in the male sex.

Now if this flesh is properly disposed over the body, we shall find the limbs and features presenting gently waving outlines, and a predominance of curved over straight lines in all the members. The proportions between the circumferences of the different members and the body will be found to vary little in persons of the same height, and to be nearly the same in persons of any height. There is in such figures an exhaustless variety included in a perfect harmony.

We made the reservation that the rules we are about to give will be nigh infallible unless a person is a victim of some disease. It is quite important to bear this in mind, for there are diseases which first manifest their presence by a change in the figure. Many persons suppose corpulence is a sure indication of excellent health. This is far from true. Certain maladies are always attended by the deposition of layers of unhealthy fat. These persons are rarely long-lived. "Fatty degeneration" is the name given to a dangerous complaint especially characterized by a tendency of the tissues to change into fat.

Often, too, corpulence is a protection thrown out by the system against some threatening disease. If the corpulence is then successfully attacked, the victory may cost the person her life. A case is recorded by Dr. Maccary where an obese child was reduced in flesh, but became ever after subject to epileptic fits. A number of instances have been recently published in medical journals, where ladies have brought on fatal disease of the kidneys by a too determinate and unwise reduction of their weight. A case came recently under our own notice, where a young lady weighing nearly two hundred pounds, entered upon the reduction of her size with great zeal, but little discretion. She succeeded, but developed in the process the seeds of hereditary consumption of the lungs. No such attempt should ever be made, therefore, until some skilful physician has not only examined for any lurking signs of disease, but has inquired carefully into the personal and family history, and, to the extent of human power, satisfied himself there is no danger.

Then, also, there are certain periods in the physical life of woman when such a proposed change should *under no circumstances* be commenced or continued. These are at puberty, during pregnancy, during nursing, and about the change of life. The reasons for this caution will be obvious to every intelligent woman.

Furthermore, the seasons of the year must be considered. The "bills of fare" that we are about to give can be better filled at one season than another, so that less self-control will be needed to follow them out.

4*

Other things being equal, that season should be chosen when the person usually feels in best health.

With these precautions, the more abrupt, decided, and total the change, the better. There is no wisdom and less satisfaction in a *gradual* reform. This change includes three points, diet, habits, and medicines. And first as to diet.

Here we can in no wise escape the mention of Banting. The pursy Englishman with his tract "On Corpulence" will figure conspicuously for some time to come in treatises on this topic. Some men of science were outraged at his presumption in trenching on their domain. They either cried out, "It is not new," or else, "It is not true." But the stubborn fact remained that the.fat old gentleman *did* grow comfortably spare.

The truth of the matter is that certain foods are much more readily converted into fat than others, and that if persons sedulously avoid such, they will gradually reduce their weight. Now it has long been known in a general way, that these articles are those which contain sugar or starch in large quantities. But when Mr. Banting paid his guinea, and expected some sound practical advice in exchange for it, the doctor either pooh-poohed at his anxiety, told him not to worry himself about his size, that it was natural at his age, and so forth; or else shook his head ponderously, and said oracularly, "Avoid saccharine and amylaceous articles of diet," disdaining any farther specification.

At length he met a medical adviser who took the pains to point out just *what* articles he should and should not eat.

It is true that any kind of food which will support life can make fat. But certain kinds make it much more rapidly than others. Then it must be remembered that a great part of what we popularly term fat is simply watery fluid in the tissues. When this is very abundant it is vulgarly called "bloat." Reduce this watery fluid, and confine the diet to such food as is least fat-making, and the problem of controlling the weight is solved.

A truce to physiology and let us to business. What the fat reader wants is no long-drawn dissertation on dietetics, carbonaceous and non-carbonaceous food, alimentation, and what not, for which she has no mind and no appetite, but a classified list of what she may and may not touch, a bill of fare ready made to her hand, well arranged and easy of reference.

We happen to be provided with just such a document, and have the honor to lay before her our

BILL OF FARE TO DECREASE IN WEIGHT.

Breakfast (from 6 to 8 A. M.).

Lean beef, mutton, game, cold fowl, or other meat, except pork, bacon, or veal.

Any fish except catfish, eels, salmon, or fresh mackerel.

Eggs boiled, dropped, or in an omelette, most of the yelk being avoided.

A small piece of ship's biscuit, gluten or bran bread, or thin dry toast from stale bread.

Coffee or tea, one cup, without milk or sugar. Russian tea is very suitable. It has a thick slice of lemon floating in the cup instead of milk or sugar.

Dinner (from 1 to 3 P. M.).

Soup—*maigre.*

Fish—of any kind, except those mentioned above, prepared plainly.

Meats—Mutton, beef, game, fowls, or any other lean meat with the exceptions mentioned above, the fat being carefully skimmed from the gravies.

Vegetables—Beans, peas, cabbages, onions, apple-sauce, tomatoes, asparagus, eggplant, or any other vegetable *except* beets, oyster plant, turnips, potatoes, carrots, rice, green peas and corn.

Gluten bread, or a small portion of bran bread.

Dessert—Fruit cooked without sugar, water-ice, cheese.

For drinks, pure water, and if accustomed to spirits, better stop them.

Supper (from 6 to 7 P. M.).

Cold meat from the dinner.

A small portion of dry toast or gluten bread, cheese, water-ice. Plain fruit without sugar. Raw tomatoes. Apple sauce without sugar. The white of dropped eggs.

Tea without milk or sugar.

We might have stated the quantities in this list, but it is unnecessary. The appetite should be satisfied, but never overloaded. Fluids of all kinds should be diminished to the lowest degree consistent with comfort. The articles of food which should be most sedulously avoided are these :—

Bread, butter, milk, sugar, potatoes sweet and white, molasses, fat meat, Indian corn, pastry, beer.

The more nearly every one of these is absolutely cut off, the more rapid will be the reduction in the weight.

One about to undertake this diet should be weighed the day she commences and once a week for several months. The obvious decrease in rotundity will cheer her in her self-denials. This happy result should be quite evident in a week's time. We promise her with the most confident air in the world, that if she will rigidly and faithfully follow out these precepts and abstain from the forbidden fruits (if we may ask so much from a daughter of Eve), she will most certainly see a cheering diminution in that period, which will regularly continue until she is no longer, with Falstaff, "out of all reasonable compass."

This bill of fare must, we repeat, be enjoyed in moderation. It is well to eat enough, for the idea so often entertained of *starving* one's self thin is foolish. Such a course cannot possibly succeed unless the health too is ruined. But it is better to eat too little than too much. If this causes a feeling of emptiness at the pit of the stomach, it can be relieved by chewing a grain or two of coffee. Like Epictetus' philosophers the corpulent "must guard and plot against themselves."

There is no great self-denial demanded from our fat friends thus far. But now we are going to be more disagreeable. We are going to criticize a number of delightful little self-indulgences. We shall not, however, be so odious as Dr. Unger, a German physician of renown. A patient once applied to him for some means to shorten his ever increasing waist-band.

" You can't do it with more honor to yourself," replied the surly old doctor, " than by studying algebra all night, and chopping wood all day."

No, we shall not go that far. We shall allow our corpulent client to sleep, but not over six or seven hours, and we stipulate for a *hard* bed. Pressure is a sovereign disperser of fat. She ought to rise early, and the first thing in the morning wash herself from head to foot with strong brine, of the temperature of the room. A handful of rock-salt to a basin of water is the proportion. She must then rub herself dry with a rough towel, or, still better, a pair of rough flesh gloves. If in a city, a Turkish or Russian bath twice a week is not amiss.

There is to be no nap at all, not a wink, during the daytime. If she feels drowsy, she should take some active exercise. Exercise it is true is not indispensable, but it is a useful assistant. We have explained that much of so-called fat is only water. This may be driven from the system by perspiration, and by the action of the kidneys and the lungs. If, therefore, in addition to the diet, daily exercise is used, the diminution will be more rapid. Riding, rowing, and parlor gymnastics may be commenced. But we know how disagreeable exercise is to the stout, so we state distinctly that the diet we have recommended is alone sufficient to reduce the size.

The bowels are to be kept loose, and for this purpose nothing is so suitable as Congress, Kissingen, Bedford, or Carlsbad water. But these must be taken in moderation, as must all other fluids.

The mind should be employed, as indolence is ever a provocative of obesity. There are always matters enough to think about or to study, if one has the will for it.

Lastly, a word is to be said about medicines. Several of these have a decided effect on the deposition of fat, and aid in dispersing it. But they are edged tools, very apt to cut those who ignorantly meddle with them. The most renowned are liquor potassæ, acetic acid, bromide of ammonium, iodide of potassium, the haloid salts of cadmium, and the fucus vesiculosus. Most of these are powerful stimulants to the secretory organs, and none of them should be used except under the supervision of a physician. Still less should any recourse be had to the patented, secret, or advertised nostrums for the reduction of corpulence. They are *without exception* perilous to the general health, or wholly inert. No medicines whatever are necessary if the diet table be strictly observed, and although we know that the use of some of the drugs we mention assists the effects of diet, they can nearly always be dispensed with.

All this time our fat friends have been crowding upon us, and we have only said a word to the spare ones. Now their turn is come. We have matter of consolation for them too. They need it, poor things. There are countries in the world where a woman ever so fat, even if she rivals the famous Daniel Lambert, who weighed seven hundred and thirty-nine pounds, will be esteemed only the more attractive. But a scrawny bony figure—this is, like poor poetry, intolerable to gods and men. The only lady who we ever heard derived advantage from such an appearance was Madame Ida Pfeiffer. She relates that somewhere in her African travels the natives had a mind to kill and eat her, but she looked so unpalatably lean and tough that the temptation was not strong enough, and thus her life was saved.

Probably if a census were taken with this object in view, we would find more persons who wish to increase their weight than there are who are anxious to decrease it. We hear more complaints from the stout, because obesity is a more troublesome condition than excessive spareness. But the latter is quite as fatal to beauty, and unquestionably far more common in the young. Even in the days of St. Chrysostom, the question "how to grow stouter" appears to have been one anxiously considered by the ladies of Antioch, where the good father preached. He was not in the least inclined to indorse this vanity, and told them one day in his sermon, that "the virtue of the body does not consist in fatness, but in the capacity of bearing torments." We do not think that in this day of wasp-like waists and tight laced figures the Saint's words would be appropriate.

Leanness like corpulence is often a family trait, and is much more frequently than that condition associated with disease. We may lay it down as a rule that when a person in seemingly good health commences to fall away in flesh, there is some lurking disorder of the nutritive system at work. Three times out of four this disorder will be found in the liver or stomach, and if taken in hand early, and treated wisely and energetically, not only will good looks but health also be rescued.

In quite a number of spare women, marriage has a singularly beneficial influence. They improve rapidly in flesh and in color. But no woman need marry for this object. We can promise her a comfortable plumpness without recourse to so risky a remedy. We explained a few pages back that some articles of food made much more fat than others. Let her live on these, and that she may do so the more readily, here is a

BILL OF FARE TO INCREASE IN FLESH.

Breakfast (8 to 10 A. M.).

Bacon, ham, sausage, pork steak, mutton or veal, with rich gravies.

Fresh fish, especially eels, catfish, trout, or salmon.

The yelks of eggs, fried, scrambled or dropped.

Buckwheat, Indian, or wheaten cakes, with plenty of butter and molasses, syrup, honey, or sugar. Fresh bread and butter.

Fried or boiled mush or grits, with butter, sugar, cream, or syrup. Fried or boiled potatoes.

Fresh milk, plain or sweetened, warm or cool, chocolate, cocoa, or coffee, with plenty of cream and sugar.

Lunch (about noon).

Eggs and milk, or fresh milk, with sweet cake, preserves, jellies, honey, bread and butter.

Dinner (about 3 P. M.).

Soup—Gumbo, okra, calf's head, mock turtle, sago.

Fish—Salmon, eels, catfish, trout, with dressing of drawn butter or cream.

Meats—Roast pig or roast pork, lamb with guava or currant jelly, fried bacon, boiled pork, roast lamb or beef (fat), roast or fried veal.

Vegetables—Ruta-baga turnips, sugar-beets, potatoes (roast or mashed with cream), parsnips, carrots, green peas and corn, salad with cream dressing, grits, rice, macaroni, vermicelli.

Dessert—Suet pudding with cream dip, tapioca or starch

pudding, arrowroot, sago, cream cakes, meringues, custards, sweetmeats, honey, nuts, bananas, sweet grapes, pastry, ice cream.

Milk or cream.

Supper (about 7 P. M.).

Bread and butter, or bread and milk, with preserves, jams, or syrup, oatmeal porridge. Mush with milk or molasses. Cold bacon or mutton.

Milk sweetened or plain. Tea with cream and sugar.

Every person must watch and weigh himself, and thus learn what articles of diet are in his individual case most fattening. Mr. Banting found from his experience that to him *sugar* was the most productive of fat. If he ate five ounces of it, he increased one pound! Dr. Stark, likewise speaking from his own knowledge, declares in favor of *suet* as that which fleshed him most rapidly. Another high authority says that *milk*, especially when taken fresh and from an Alderney cow, is superior to anything else. If one can drink three or four pints of it a day, an increase in weight is as certain, and perhaps more certain, than by swallowing cod-liver oil. *Starch* in the form of arrowroot, sago, tapioca, or farina, is equally lauded by others.

To be avoided on the other hand are: pickles, vinegars, highly spiced food, sour wines or fruits, acid vegetables.

To decrease in size a diet chiefly animal is required;

to increase, a diet largely vegetable is most efficient. Of vegetables, the roots are as a rule fattening, while those which ripen above ground have not such an effect.

There is no need to stuff one's self with these appetizing dishes. Remember it is not the quantity but the kind of food, and its ready conversion into flesh that are demanded. It is essential that the digestion be kept in perfect order, therefore an overloaded stomach is a positive injury.

In some parts of Asia, where a considerable *embonpoint* is deemed essential to beauty, the art of fattening damsels "for the trade" has been carried to a high degree of perfection. They sleep long and late on soft beds, and they avoid violent exercise or disturbing thoughts. They bathe in lukewarm water, and take while in the bath a broth made from fat chickens boiled with rice or with arrowroot. On leaving the water they are softly rubbed down with scented vegetable oils, such as pure olive oil boiled with gum benzoin, which not only preserves it from rancidity but imparts to it a rich aroma. The oil prevents the watery fluid from passing out in the perspiration, and softens the outer layer of the skin. They drink moderately of a sweet mixture of honey and water, and take daily a preparation of the castor bean, which slightly moves the bowels and increases the appetite.

All these details are not applicable with us, but this

is the true method to pursue. Irregular hours of rest or for meals, eating between meals, anxiety, overwork, severe exercise, these are sure to maintain a condition of leanness.

As for the various drugs which have been suggested, their use had better be confined to simply maintaining the regularity of the natural functions. Some of the mineral waters of Germany and our own country have acquired a reputation for increasing the flesh, probably owing to the fillip they give to the digestion. These are Töplitz, Gastein, and Landeck, in Germany, and the White Sulphur and chalybeate springs in this country.

There is danger that such a bill of fare as this latter may make some people "bilious," and others gouty, if long persisted in. These tendencies may be combated by a careful attention to the regularity of the functions of the body. A glass of Congress or Bedford water, every morning before breakfast, is a salutary draught in the former case, and in the latter an equal amount of Gettysburg water will be found of service. The latter contains, it is said, a small quantity of the substance lithia, from which it derives its virtues.

Any one will more willingly run these dangers of over-feeding than adopt the method of increasing flesh recommended by Galen and some other physicians of the olden time. This was nothing more nor less than a sound flogging every day or two! This old Roman writer tells us that in his day the slave dealers whipped their chattels soundly, so as to get them in fine, plump condition for the market. Then, too, it was so much cheaper than mutton and corn! "No doubt," says Dr. John Bell, in his work on Beauty, "such flagellation tends to increase the circulation at the surface, and give tone to languid muscles;" but no one need be afraid that we are proposing to recommend it.

THE NECK AND BUST.

THE PROPER FORM OF THE NECK.

WE believe it is Burke who somewhere says, "that of all the beautiful objects in nature, none surpasses the well-moulded neck of woman." There are, indeed, a softness of outline and a harmony of motion about it worthy to challenge the admiration of philosophers.

In length it should be one-half the height of the head from the level of the chin to the summit, and at its narrowest part should have twice the circumference of the wrist.

Through the neck the great vessels pass to the head, and the spinal column conveys the sensations of all parts of the body to the brain, where resides the intellect. Therefore it is of marked significance in reading character, and reveals much to the physiognomist, and also to the physician. The crises which take place in the physical life of woman, and her liability

(55)

to certain serious accidents are portended by the shape
of her neck. When it is full in front it signifies a
plethoric constitution, liable to the accidents which
arise from a too sanguineous habit. At about the age
of forty a deposit of fat occurs low down at the back
of the neck, over the vertebræ, forming sometimes a
small prominent mass, which reveals the age more certainly than words.

WRY-NECK AND GOITRE.

The most common defects in the contour of the
neck are owing to irregular action of the muscles
drawing it over to one side, or to the peculiar swelling of the glands known as goitre.

Children not unfrequently seem unable to hold the
head erect for any length of time. It drops forward
on the chest or to one side. Others have " wry-neck,"
in which complaint the head is drawn forcibly toward
one shoulder by a shortening of the muscles.

Such conspicuous disfigurements as these should
have prompt attention, the more so as they are readily
remedied by proper means. It has been recently discovered that an injection of the active principle of
belladonna beneath the skin often acts with great
efficiency, but other cases require surgical appliances
and sometimes an operation, quite too formidable to
be described here.

Goitre is a swelling in the front part of the neck.

It grows slowly, but finally arrives at such a size that it constitutes a serious deformity. To a slight extent it is by some regarded as an advantage, giving the neck a full and rounded appearance. In Switzerland, where it is very prevalent, it is indeed considered quite essential to beauty. A traveller in that country relates that once he heard some Swiss ladies commenting on the personal appearance of a fine-looking Englishman. "What a handsome man he would be," exclaimed one of them, "if he only had a goitre!" Doubtless the Englishman was well content at the absence of this additional charm.

In this country we have seen quite a number of persons with a tendency to this deformity, especially in districts where limestone water had to be used. This is one of its supposed causes, but in one case now under our treatment, and in others we have seen, it is undoubtedly hereditary. It occurs more frequently in females than in males, and is apt to make its first appearance about the period of puberty. Although not a dangerous, it is a most objectionable complaint on account of the deformity it causes, and, moreover, when the tumor increases in size, it gives rise to many inconveniences by pressure on the large bloodvessels in the neck, and renders the voice harsh and coarse.

When taken early, it can be cured almost without fail, but if allowed to run on for many years the sub-

stance of the swelling often changes into a bony sub
stance, to remove which is beyond the reach of art. It
is important, therefore, that parents should be on the
watch, and call the attention of the family physician
to any fulness of the neck, at an early enough period
to allow him to administer those remedies which at
this epoch of the disease are almost certain to remove
it promptly and permanently. Change of climate is
advantageous but not necessary.

THE SHOULDERS AND CHEST.

Rounded, sloping, regular shoulders are indispensable to beauty, and they are the more important as
full-dress frequently requires them to be displayed.
They should be equal in height, and slope symmetrically in graceful curves from the base of the neck to
the summit of the chest.

One of their most frequent faults is to be square
instead of curved—to start almost horizontally from
the base of the neck on either side. For this deformity—it is nothing less than a deformity—most
women have nobody but themselves to thank. In
four cases out of five it has been brought about by too
close-fitting corsets, which press the shoulder-blades
behind, and collar bones in front, too far upward, and
thus ruin the appearance of the shoulders. When
this ugliness is once acquired, it is by no means easy

to do away with it. An avoidance of the cause, and appropriate gymnastic exercises promise the most.

We have previously remarked (page 29) that writers and painters, sitting as they usually do, with one arm elevated, holding the pen or brush, and the other at rest or nearly so, almost certainly come to have one shoulder higher than the other. This gives the whole bust a one-sided appearance, eminently unpleasing. Young ladies who are of a literary turn of mind, therefore, or are artistically inclined, and yet whose devotion to ideal and intellectual beauty does not quite lead them to the neglect of that physical beauty which nature has bestowed on them, will act wisely to correct this tendency by constant care and exercise.

A bad habit or some local weakness occasionally leads to holding one shoulder slightly in advance of the other, or to bringing them both forward, giving the chest a hollow, "dished" appearance, exactly the reverse of what it should have.

Such a conformation is the more unsightly in woman, as she has naturally a more prominent chest than man. Her collar-bones are longer, and her shoulders are pressed by them farther outward and backward, in order to give room for spreading that banquet for an unborn guest, which it is her duty and her destiny to furnish. There should be no salient bones or angles, but the outline should sweep in a series of gentle curves from the neck downward, each slightly in advance of the other, until they merge in the semicircular arcs which define the chief and highest beauty of woman—the breasts.

There should especially be no hollows under the collar-bones, over the apex of the lungs. When present, they signify more than a want of comeliness—they betoken the danger, if not the actual presence, of that fatal and frequent disease, pulmonary consumption. It is precisely in that spot that the physician searches for the earliest warnings of this malady, and who can think of mortal, perishable beauty, when he sees the stealthy hand of death already claiming these charms?

THE BREASTS AND WAIST.

Symbols of maternal love and fruitfulness, deeply in sympathy with all feminine instincts and sensations, well-formed breasts have ever been considered by artists essential requisites of beauty. They should be firm and elastic, rising from the chest true hemispheres in shape, situated neither too high nor too low. The distance from the nipple to the lower edge of the collar bone of the same side should equal that from one nipple to the other, which, in turn, should be precisely one-fourth of the circumference of the chest at their level. The space between the bases should equal the diameter of the base of either.

Yet alas! in this artificial life of ours, how often

have we seen a female bust that answered these demands? Or rather, have we ever seen one? "I never knew before I came to Egypt," says Lady Duff-Gordon in her recent book of travels, "what a female breast is. We never see it in Europe." Neither do we in America, without it may be in some vigorous young country girl, who has grown up in ignorance of the arts which thwart nature.

Not that taste approves now-a-days that fashion which early in the last century prevailed in France and Spain. Then, in accordance with the mode of the day which despised everything which was spontaneous and delighted in the artificial and the abnormal, the type of elegance was a perfectly flat breast. The fine ladies used to wear from early girlhood circular plates of lead, strapped firmly against their breasts, in order to cause their absorption. Of course, these noble dames were utterly disqualified from nursing their own children, but this troubled them little.

Unfortunately, modern ladies, in their desire *not* to appear flat-breasted, are guilty of precisely the same violation of nature's laws. From early youth they wear pads of hair or cotton, which they fasten over the breasts with straps and the corset, so as to make a "form." These act in a similar manner as the plates of lead. The breasts are flattened, distorted, partly absorbed, and often completely unfitted for their natural function. The nipples are drawn in, and be-

6

come retracted and tender. Physicians daily encounter the evil results of such folly, and many a mother has to forego the sweet toil of nursing her own children by having injured her breasts at the behest of fashion.

If something of the kind *must* be worn to make up the form in obedience to the mode, let it be the hollow hemispheres of vulcanized India-rubber or of woven wire, which are at once firm and elastic, which exert no pressure on the gland itself, yet give a perfect and fascinating outline. They are now manufactured of various sizes to suit, and may be had in this and other cities.

An instrument, which seems to have claims as a promoter of health and beauty, has been invented for improving the shape of the breast. It is a bowl of glass to which is fitted a stopcock. The air is exhausted by means of an air syringe, and a flow of blood to the part follows. It is highly likely that this device would be of considerable service, and that the breasts would be rendered much more shapely, and better adapted to fulfil their functions. The theory of the instrument is philosophical, and if used regularly for a sufficient time must certainly restore the organs in great measure to their proper shape, size, and function. As the breasts are delicate, and liable to various inflammatory diseases, proper caution should be observed not to injure them by too violent applications, and whenever tenderness is produced, the instrument should be laid aside until the sensation subsides. After having had them once explained, any one can use these vacuum cups with readiness and safety.

The opposite trouble, breasts of inordinate and inconvenient magnitude, also occurs. We know a lady, who with every opportunity and faculty to shine in social life, has denied herself to general society for years, on account of this malformation. In her case, as in most, it is associated with an undue mental sensitiveness regarding her form, which is a constant source of unnecessary distress to her.

Sometimes the overgrowth is astonishing. Professor Gross, of Philadelphia, mentions one case where each breast weighed fifteen pounds, and not long since, a case was operated on in Paris, where each weighed nearly thirty pounds. When the excess in size is moderate, the breast can readily be reduced by constant inunction of an ointment of cadmium or iodine, the administration of iodide of potassium internally, and especially by long-continued, firmly-applied bandages of adhesive plaster. This treatment must be adopted under the supervision of a medical adviser, as ignorant management may very easily lead to severe suffering.

Those who would improve the contour of the chest, can do so with great certainty and in a short space of time as follows: Loosen the clothing, and standing erect, throw the shoulders well back, the hands behind, and the breast forward. In this position, draw slowly as deep an inspiration as possible, and retain it by an increased effort for a few seconds. Then breathe it gradually forth. After a few natural breaths, repeat the long inspiration. Let this be done for fifteen or twenty minutes every day, and in six weeks' time a perceptible increase in the diameter of the chest and in its prominence will be very evident.

The breasts are liable to many diseases, especially to tumors, which destroy their shape. But these come strictly within the province of the surgeon, and need not be mentioned here. So, too, the breasts require especial attention during and after confinement, while nursing, and at weaning, both to preserve their health and their beauty, but as these points have been spoken of at length, in the " Physical Life of Woman," to which we have referred, the repetition is superfluous. We would, however, call attention to the fact, that if a woman does not intend to nurse her child, she should, to preserve her breast in shape, dry up her milk at the outset by artificial means.

The lower part of the chest is more capacious than the upper, and incloses some of the most important organs of the economy. At the waist, the body should have the least circumference. While this is true, it is an absurd and ugly fashion. not sanctioned by any rule of art, and in positive opposition to the laws of health and beauty, to compress, fasten, and lace it down to that "wasp-like waist," against which artists and physicians have so long and so vainly protested.

The circumference of the waist in a woman five feet high should not be less than twenty-five inches, and from this it should increase half an inch in circumference for every additional inch in height, so that a woman five feet eight inches high should measure twenty-nine inches around the waist, of course without the clothing.

The result of any greater compression than this is disastrous in every respect. We have already shown how it spoils the shape of the shoulders, and flattens and displaces the breasts. Were this all, it might pass. But far more serious consequences arise. The lungs are cramped and cannot expand. The blood, in consequence, is not purified, the complexion soon becomes muddy, the lips pale or purple, and if there is any tendency to consumption, it is promptly developed. The pressure downward is equally productive of harm. A physician who pays special attention to diseases of women, recently told us that four-fifths of the cases of uterine complaint which he had to treat in unmarried women were directly traceable to this violent and unnatural pressure upon the contents of the abdomen. Our own experience convinces us that his statement is hardly overdrawn. With these consequences plainly staring them in the face, it is scarcely credible that women, who wish to preserve either their health or their beauty, will deliberately continue to take so certain a means of destroying both as this compression of the waist.

If support is what is needed, a light steel brace is infinitely preferable, more cleanly, more durable, and more healthful. Excellent ones can be bought in all our large cities. If it is desired to reduce an exuberant form, we have already laid down the rules for that. If the object is to "make up the figure," those have the best success who, like the Italian ladies, depend on the arrangement of the dress and a careful carriage, and not on forcing the body into unnatural positions.

There has been said so much on this topic by physicians that it is probably a tiresome one to readers. Perhaps they are ready to paraphrase Shakspeare and exclaim against the doctors as "fellows of —— iteration." We make our attack on the custom from a new quarter, and in the interests of beauty itself demand that respect be paid to fundamental laws of health. Unless we are implicitly obeyed here, we cannot keep our promise that our readers shall remain beautiful longer than they are young.

THE HEAD, FACE, AND EXPRESSION.

THE SHAPE OF THE HEAD.

THE head is that part of the body which distinguishes the noble races and individuals from those which are ignoble. Its highest type is never seen except in the most civilized families of the white race, where, by its symmetrical proportions, it manifests the superiority of this over other varieties of our species.

It should appear as a perfect oval, whether looked at from above downward, or from in front. Its height should be a little less than one-eighth of the whole height of the person. The greatest diameter should extend from the forehead to the back of the skull above the neck, the shortest from one temple to the other. The two hemispheres should be perfectly alike, and the curve of the summit regular and even.

As the seat of the brain and the mental faculties, it has been supposed that by an examination of the outside of the head, some conclusion could be formed of the character and abilities of the person. Under the name of phrenology, this popular notion was cultivated diligently some years ago by itinerant lecturers, but of late the business seems to have fallen off. We well remember a friend at college, now holding a prominent and responsible position as an educator, who pointed out to us with great satisfaction a small lump about the middle of his forehead, which he confidently maintained had grown there since he had addressed himself to the study of history. Since then, like others, he has lost faith in Gall and Spurzheim.

To confess the truth, we know absolutely nothing about the functions of the various parts of the brain. The least difficult theory is that the anterior third is the seat of the intellectual faculties, the middle third controls nutrition and emotion, while the posterior third governs muscular action, and the sentiments of reproduction.

No doubt the capacity of the skull, that is to say, the size of the brain, has a close connection with the mental power. But it is very far from true that a large head is a guarantee of a strong intellect. Daniel Webster had the largest head in Congress, and John Randolph the smallest, but the latter was very little inferior to the former in close, logical argument, and was much quicker at repartee and satire. Women have somewhat smaller heads than men in proportion to their height, but in many respects women are unquestionably superior to men.

The symmetry of the two sides of the head is not always preserved. The celebrated anatomist, Bichat, who, though dying at the early age of thirty-one, had already achieved world-wide fame by his medical discoveries, was wont to maintain that in such instances the mental faculties must be impaired. But he proved in his own person that his view was untenable, for on an examination of his body after death, one hemisphere of the brain was found decidedly larger than the other.

Some years ago we had under our care a child which was in excellent health, but in whom the left side of the head was larger than the right. We counselled delay, and since then the skull has gradually assumed a more correct shape, and the mind is entirely sound. In such instances, unless nature acted soon, we should not hesitate to use judiciously regulated pressure. Every one knows there are some savage tribes who flatten or elongate the heads of their infants without ill results. At a tender age the bones of the skull will readily adapt themselves to a mould, and that without injury to the delicate parts within.

A common disease of children, causing sad deformity of the head, is known as "water on the brain," or hydrocephalus. This is a serious complaint, and requires prompt medical assistance.

The *forehead* in women should be rather low and broad. This was the rule of the ancient artists. It was thought that a high forehead gives a bold or else a shrewish expression to the countenance. Nevertheless, we admire none of the " foreheads villainous low," denoting a limited or a perverse intellect. The height from the bridge of the nose should exactly equal the length of the nose.

In some persons the hair grows down upon the forehead, destroying its contour and beauty. This may be remedied by carefully removing the hairs, which are generally thin and fine, by one of the depilatories to be mentioned hereafter. Charlotte Bremer, in her Life of her sister, Frederica Bremer, relates that this was one of the girlish troubles of the gifted authoress, and her mother often regretted the disfigurement. One day Frederica cut off the hair around her forehead with the scissors. Her mother, not at once perceiving what she had been about, remarked in the course of the day, " Why, Frederica, your forehead is not so low after all." This delighted her daughter, but soon the hairs commenced to reappear, stiff and bristly. But with heroic perseverance, Frederica pulled them out, one after another, with a pair of tweezers, until she had achieved that fine high forehead, which those who saw her in her visit to this country may remember.

A retreating forehead is always a marplot to beauty,

and gives one the aspect of fatuity or half-idiocy. One of the Indian tribes in our western country dislike it so much that they press the skull of the child forward, so that they all have a highly intellectual appearance.

Wrinkles and spots on the forehead we shall treat of in the chapter on the skin.

A forehead broad in proportion to its height gives an air of dignity and queenliness, always much admired. There is an ancient Spanish poem dating from some time in the Middle Ages called "The Thirty Beauties of Woman," one of the lines of which is:—

"Tres anchas, los pechos, la frente, y el entrecejo."

"Three parts should be broad: the breast, the forehead, and the space between the eyebrows."

This dictum is strictly in accordance with the laws of ideal proportion. The head, in every view of it, should appear larger in the superior part, and gradually diminish as it descends. The beauty of the face, observes one of the great critics of art (Winkelman), depends largely on the angle which the line of the forehead seen in profile makes with the line of the nose. The greater the angle, in other words, the nearer the profile approaches a straight line, the more majestic and soft is the general expression. This observation, founded on a long contemplation of Greek art, is eminently true.

THE FACE, AND EXPRESSION.

The face, like the head, should form nearly an oval when viewed from in front. Its height, from the upper border of the forehead to the base of the chin, should be three times the length of the nose, measured along its base, and equal a line drawn along the eyebrows, from the outer extremity of one to that of the other.

A line drawn from the cavity of the ear to the most prominent part of the upper jaw, should meet another line drawn from the central and highest point of the forehead to the same point, almost at right angles; that is, the upper jaw should project very little or not at all beyond the line of the forehead. This angle is called the "facial angle," and is deemed of much importance in studying heads.

The lower part of the profile should neither recede nor project more than the upper, and whether regarded from half, quarter, or full face, the outline should present soft curves, not abrupt angles, or sudden depressions. The bones, which here approach nearer the surface than in other parts of the body, should be well clothed with flesh, but not to the extent of hiding their general forms.

It is easy to lay down these rules one after another, but how are we to conform to them? What aid can cosmetic science here offer to one not gifted by nature with a handsome face?

Directly, perhaps, there is little to be done, but indirectly a great deal. For, after all, it is not these mathematical diagrams which we have been describing that make up beauty. It is *expression*, the soul, if you will, shining through its mortal coil.

And here we have no longer to do with unyielding bone and solid flesh, but with material infinitely more plastic than even the tempered clay in which the sculptor forms his model. The vast majority of persons are neither repulsive nor beautiful in feature, and it is the *expression of their faces* which grants or denies them popularity and success. Therefore this is a most weighty branch of our theme, and all the more so because expression is very much under our own control, if we only know it.

For what makes expression? Chiefly the action of certain muscles of the face. Why it is that joy or sadness, love or hate, fear or anger, should each call into action a particular muscle on this prominent and visible part of the human frame, we do not know. But the fact can be shown· by this strange experiment: Connect the poles of an electric battery with these separate muscles on the face of a corpse, and you will see the ghastly spectacle of the passions of rage, of mirth, of lust, of hate, one after another brought into horrid relief on the countenance of death.

The habitual use of one of these muscles above the other, enlarges it, and leaves on the countenance marks

7

which observers ever associate with the passion. No one but can recall some face where petulance, or grief, or pride, has left indelible imprints. Like a mirror, the unguarded expression tells tales of all that is passing within us. The skilled eye reads at a glance the passing thought. This authentic anecdote is told of that expert diplomatist and profound student of human nature, the Prince de Talleyrand. For a short time he was an exile to this country, and resided in New York city. One day he was walking with a friend along the Battery, in those early times a fashionable promenade. Turning and scanning closely the face of his companion, he suddenly exclaimed: "Wretch! you are planning to assassinate me!" Detected by what seemed a superhuman insight, his pretended friend threw himself at his feet, and confessed that he was proposing in his mind to murder and rob the prince.

As men are only too apt to indulge the unpleasant rather than the pleasant emotions, it has ever been advised to control the features, and whether in company or alone, by a mental effort to prevent our thoughts from acting on our expression. *Volto sciolto, pensieri stretti*, the countenance open, the thoughts shut, is the Italian's motto; and our own Shakspeare sings of his love—

"In many's looks the false heart's history,
  Is writ, in moods and frowns and wrinkles strange;
  But heaven in thy creation did decree,

That in thy face sweet love should ever dwell ;
Whate'er thy thoughts or thy heart's workings be,
Thy looks do nothing thence but sweetness tell.
   How like Eve's apple doth thy beauty grow
   If thy sweet virtue answer not thy show ?"

It should be the aim of every one thus to become "the lords and owners of their faces," and it is in the power of every one, not irrecoverably wedded to some grimace, to do so.

The first step is to break at once from any of those bad practices which the French call *tics*, such as winking violently or with one eye, frowning, sniffing, or "turning up the nose," thrusting the tongue into the cheek, pointing the lips, pursing up the mouth or letting it loll open, opening widely the eyes, wagging the head, grinning, and so forth. Remember to obey this rule, which indeed is worthy to be classed in the Decalogue of good breeding as well as of cosmetics:—

Never "make faces" while you are talking.

No *tic* is more certain to damage a pretty face than this twisting and contortion of the features. Cultivate placidity of expression, and rest assured that there is no danger of vacancy of countenance. On a calm face the passing emotions mirror themselves with a pleasing variety, like clouds on the surface of some unruffled mere; but with jerking and twitching muscles, the emotions are broken and lost, like the reflections of those same clouds on a wind-scourged sea.

There are some persons who, when they weep, screw up the countenance in such an unheard-of manner, that it forces the looker-on to be amused, even while he sympathizes; and there are others who, when they laugh, do such violence to all the laws of good looks that it is enough to make the judicious weep. We have heard not a few public speakers, worthy men, too, who forfeited half their power by grimacing in the pulpit like a mime on the stage. School girls often learn to chew with their mouths open, and with an exertion of the muscles of the jaws quite super-fluous, even though, like Sancho Panza, they chew on both sides at once.

All such habits are enemies to beauty, and are also inconsistent with good breeding. They must be reformed, not indifferently, but at once, and altogether.

The reform must not stop here. It must extend to the mind itself. Violent passion, or long indulgence of any one emotion, is not less hurtful to the face than it is to the mind. Serenity of disposition is the true Fountain of Youth.

We live in the ancient city of Penn, and many a visitor has asked us: "Doctor, why is it these old Quaker ladies whom I meet in the streets have such fresh complexions, and so few wrinkles? Is it their poke-bonnets which keep off the sun? Or have they some secret?"

No, madam, it is not their poke-bonnets, as you are

pleased to term them, nor have they any secret, or at least it is an open one. But it is very stuff o' the conscience with them to yield to no inordinate emotion, to be temperate in all things, and to hold under strict command their bodies and their minds. You see they are rewarded by prolonged good looks; and if you step around to an insurance office you will learn their chance of long life is notably better than that of the rest of us.

Vacancy or stolidity of expression, though less intolerable than the perpetual twitching we have just described, should be shunned with equal care, and can be conquered with as certain success, if one sets about it diligently. It is easy to appear interested, or merry, or sad, when we are so.

Not a few women and many a young man are annoyed by a tendency to *blush* on slight occasion. The tell-tale blood mantles the cheeks and forehead at most inopportune moments, and seems quite beyond the control of the mind. The utmost exertion of volition does not hinder it. In some constitutions no endeavor, no custom of society can overcome it.

Count Alexandre de Tilly had been page to Queen Marie Antoinette, and had lived all his life in the best circles; but he confesses in his "Memoirs" that this difficulty had been insurmountable. "I verily believe," he says, "that if any one were abruptly and in public to say to me: 'Count, I accuse you of conspiring to murder the Khan of Persia,' my blushes and embarrassment would convict me."

Diligent cultivation of self-control is the unsatisfactory and yet the only suggestion which occurs to us to offer.

THE EYES, EYEBROWS, EYELASHES, AND THE SENSE OF SIGHT.

PROPER FORM AND COLOR OF THE EYE.

NO feature of the face is more expressive than the eye, none is more important to have under command, and to use to the best advantage. Of all senses that of sight is most valuable to us, and provides us the most gratifications. It can supply to an astonishing extent the lack of the sense of hearing. A lady recently told us that some years since she was introduced to, and conversed for an hour with, the wife of the celebrated Professor M., so well known for his discoveries in electricity. What was her astonishment afterwards to learn that that lady was entirely deaf, but had maintained a conversation for that length of time with a stranger without making an error, simply by observing the movements of the mouth and the expression!

The eyes should divide the upper from the middle

third of the face. They should be horizontal, and of a color to correspond with the complexion and the hair. In size they should be medium, and neither sunken nor prominent. Their motion should be free, slow rather than jerky, and always in the same axis, that is, they should not be in the least cross-eyed. They should be bright but not glittering, moist but not languishing, clear but not sharp. As Tennyson elegantly expresses it :—

> "Eyes not down-dropt nor over bright, but fed
> With the clear-pointed flame of chastity,
> Clear without heat, undying, tended by
> Pure vestal thoughts in the translucent flame
> Of the still spirit."

They should be strong enough to read the type in which this book is printed at a distance of four or five feet, and in form, position, color, size, and power, the one should exactly correspond with the other.

THE EYEBROWS.

The eyebrows are very significant of character and emotion. The Latin writer Pliny supposed that a portion of the soul had its dwelling there, and the German historian Herder says that the arched eyebrow is the rainbow of peace, but when contracted it is the strung bow of strife.

Their beauty consists in having them moderately thick, especially at the inner third, the outer extremity tapering to a point with soft, silken, regular hairs, of a color a shade darker than the hair of the head, *slightly* curved upwards, separated on the bridge of the nose, and with their edges clearly defined against the skin.

In some persons the eyebrows join above the nose. According to Goethe, this is indicative of a sensuous nature. It impresses one disagreeably, as it gives the appearance of a perpetual frown. Nevertheless, there are some nations, the Turks and Moors, for instance, who esteem it a beauty. When their women do not have it naturally, it is imitated by dyeing the intervening space with a preparation called *surmè*, compounded of galls and antimony. As Americans do not approve of this opinion, it is more pertinent to inquire how the obnoxious hairs may be removed. This can readily be done either by the tweezers, or, what is much less painful, by one of the depilatories we shall mention in the chapter on hair.

When the eyebrows are irregular and bristly, the offending hairs may be maintained in their proper place by adhesive pomade, or cut close to the skin one at a time, or removed entirely if they are superfluous. It is not well to trim the eyebrow generally, as it makes it coarse, and in using the tweezers great care must be taken not to pull hairs which ought to remain.

When it is desired to thicken or strengthen them, two or three drops of oil of cajuput may be gently rubbed into the skin every other night; but here, and *always* when wiping them, the rubbing should be in the direction of the hair, from the nose outward, and *never* in the reverse direction.

When it is intended to deepen their hue, it should not be done by a dye, but with a pencil of dark pomatum, which allows the greatest accuracy of application, and has no influence on the skin or eyes; or by means of a needle smoked over the flame of a candle, which is equally innocent, but less permanent.

THE EYELIDS AND EYELASHES.

The eyelids should neither be widely separated nor half-closed. The former habit gives a scared, uneasy look, damaging to the repose of beauty; the latter, either a sleepy or a sensual expression, equally far from the ideal of art. The half-closed lids are characteristic of indulgence, and seem adapted, says an elegant writer on æsthetics, "to diminish or partially to exclude the excess of those sensations which make even pleasure painful." All the pupil should be visible, but none of the white of the eye, either above or below it.

The lids are subject to various disfiguring complaints, most common of which are a redness and swelling of their margins, with more or less discharge, especially during the night. This is called *blear-eye*, or "lippitudo," and when more severe, "psorophthalmia." Sometimes it is attended with a burning and itching sensation, the edges of the lid become ulcerated and sore, and the eyelashes fall out. Frequently it arises from a tendency to scrofula, and from improperly using, or violently rubbing the eyes. When from any temporary cause. this affection can be cured by touching the margin of the lid with a little of the following preparation on the point of a camel-hair pencil, night and morning:—

Take—

Red oxide of mercury	one part ;
Glycerine (chemically pure)[1]	one part ;
Lard (free of salt)	three parts.

Mix thoroughly and keep in a cool place. Besides using this, wash the eyelid with tepid warm water, several times during the day.

If, however, blear-eye is connected with an enfeebled or scrofulous constitution, a thorough course of medical treatment is necessary.

That common annoyance *a stye* often causes disproportionate pain and trouble. It is a small, inflamed tumor on the edge of the lid. If taken *early*, they can be backened by being touched with a solid stick of nitrate of silver, but after a day or two, they must be

[1] Whenever glycerine is applied to any part of the body where there is hair, care must be taken to have it *chemically pure*, as otherwise the salts of lime, one of its most common impurities, will injure and finally destroy the hair bulbs, and cause baldness, dropping of the eyelashes, etc.

let run their course, hastened by a light poultice of slippery-elm bark. Those persons who suffer from a constant recurrence of them, one after another, should seek medical advice, as they require constitutional treatment.

A much more serious disfigurement is, when the margin of the eyelid inclines inward, or, what is worse, turns inside out. The latter is called "ectropion," and presents a most unsightly spectacle. It can only be remedied by a surgical operation.

Sometimes a portion of the skin of the nose projects over the inner angles of the eyes, imparting a coarse look to the face. Here, too, the knife of the surgeon is the only means that promises any relief.

Half-closed eyes occasionally arise from a difficulty of raising the upper lids. This is an obstinate and troublesome nervous complaint, and is not to be escaped by simple procedures.

Many a lady is disgusted with herself after a night at a ball-room or some unusual watching, or at certain periodical seasons, to find a dark blue line beneath her eyes, the sure indication of excessive excitement of the system. Gladly would she avail herself of any simple means to conceal it. We shall tell her, in confidence, how it may be done.

In London and Paris, where wild young clerks are apt to acquire a black eye occasionally in their nocturnal rambles. which might cost them their positions if the head of their houses were to notice it, there is a class of artists whose avocation it is to conceal the trace of such untoward accidents. For minor discolorations such as we are now speaking of, they employ the following method: Take a little precipitated French chalk in impalpable powder, rub it on the part, and gently blow or dust off the loose particles. Then apply a little of the same powder very slightly tinted with carmine, dusting in the same manner. Clear the edges of the eyelashes with a pencil, and tone down the outer margin of the dusted portion, so that it insensibly merges into the surrounding skin. Yet such is the vagary of the mode, that *les lionnes* of the Parisian *demi-monde* actually cultivate these dark circles beneath the eyes, to give themselves a dissolute, *effrenée* appearance.

Puffed and swollen eyelids are very common in old age and with certain complaints. Stimulant applications locally, and tonic internal treatment, will often help them materially.

Eyes apparently too small sometimes owe this defect to a too close union of the lids at the outer angle. A simple and almost painless surgical operation will readily remove this difficulty, and it should always be resorted to.

The *eyelashes* next demand our attention. They add vastly to the expression of the eye. Especially should women with light-colored, weak, or watery

8

eyes, aim to have them long, regular, silken, and dark. They can do so if they wish.

In the first place, they should see that the lid is healthy, free from minute scales at its margin, not red or everted, with no tendency to be glued to the other lid at rising in the morning. The eyelashes should then be examined one by one, and any which are split, or crooked, or feeble, should be trimmed with a pair of sharp scissors. The base of the lashes should be anointed nightly with a minute quantity of oil of cajuput on the top of a camel's-hair brush, and the examination and trimming repeated every month. If this is judiciously carried out for a few months, the result will be gratifying.

Occasionally one or several of the eyelashes grow inward, irritating the eye and ultimately injuring the sight. The only cure is to have the offending hairs extracted by the tweezers, and if they grow again to cauterize the spot with the point of a fine needle.

The odalisques of the Orient color the eyelashes with a preparation called "Kohol," which is a poisonous salt of antimony, likely to harm the eye, and, therefore, objectionable. A little Indian ink, especially that of Japanese manufacture, dissolved in water and carefully applied, answers the same purpose, and is harmless.

The brilliancy of the eye depends very much on the closeness, length, and hue of the lashes. When skil-

fully disposed and slightly darkened, if need be, they
lend a brightness and beauty altogether unexpected
to the plainest eyes. An excellent and harmless preparation to shade them a glossy dark, yet not an unnatural hue, is what is called "frankincense black." It
is made thus:—

Take—

> Frankincense, resin, pitch, of each   half an ounce;
> Gum mastic   quarter of an ounce.

Mix, and drop on red hot charcoals. Receive the fumes
in a large funnel, and a black powder will adhere to its
sides. Mix this with the fresh juice of elder berries
(or cologne water will do), and apply with a fine
camel-hair brush.

All these operations on the eyelids and eyelashes
should be performed by a second person, lest the eye
should be inadvertently injured.

THE EYE.

The beauty of the eye itself depends on its color, its
brightness, and its expression. All of these are more
or less under our control.

The white of the eye should be pure and pearly. It
is apt to become yellow in diseases connected with the
digestive organs or the liver, a bluish white in scrofulous and consumptive constitutions, and streaked with
minute red veins in those who are given to excess in
food or drink, or to violent fits of passion. The popular

mind associates the "red eye" so closely with intemperance that it has become a slang term for bad whiskey. Now, it is evident, discolorations from all these causes are in part or wholly under our own command, and that we can escape them if we will.

The pupil of the eye should suit in hue the hair and complexion. A blue eye and black hair are even more in discord than a dark eye and light hair. The latter is, indeed, esteemed by some a charm. But the color of the pupil cannot be changed by any process known to art. In elderly persons, and in those suffering from heart disease, it loses its natural tinge and changes to a dull brown.

We shall not give any tedious directions about preserving the eyes in health. It is not necessary. All there is to do is to wash them morning and evening in cool, pure water, and dry them *gently* with a soft towel, wiping them toward the nose, for in the corner nearest the nose is the outlet of the various humors secreted by the eye.

Then there is a word to be said about crying. The tears are constantly being secreted by the eye, and it is only when they are so abundant that they cannot all pass through the outlet we have just spoken of that they overflow on the cheeks. We are, in fact, ever weeping salt tears, even in our most joyous moments. Apart from the contortion of the features which usually accompanies crying. the excessive action of the tear glands soon weakens and dims the eye—

"Grief, that's beauty's canker."

The celebrated Venetian, Louis Cornaro, who ruined his constitution by excesses when young, but, by devoting himself to the care of his health, lived to be over a hundred years old, lays it down as essential to sound health not to indulge in grief. He adds, with evident satisfaction, that he had so happily cultivated himself in this respect that the death of his best friend hardly disturbed him!

Cornaro was equal to a French countess, mentioned in one of the *Mémoires* of the last century. A friend paid her a visit of condolence after the death of her husband, and advised her to give free vent to her tears.

"What!" exclaimed the lady, "would you have me double my loss? That would be to lose my beauty as well as my husband!"

A weak eye is very rarely a pretty one, so that it behooves every one to preserve the sight for a twofold reason. Reading or sewing by a light too bright or too dim, at twilight, or in a darkened room is very injurious. So is the common habit of reading when lying down. *Always* sit up to read.

One of the most curious freaks of fashion is that which introduced eyeglasses as a part of the outfit of fops and belles. An optician in one of our large cities informs us that he manufactures and sells numbers of eye-glasses with plane glass! They are carried merely as something "nobby," excellent wherewith to "ogle a party."

The fashion is not new. There is a very amusing old book called "The Ladies' Travels in Spain," written by an English lady of noble birth, who resided at the Court of Madrid about 1670. She gives many queer particulars of social customs there, and among others, that it was the fashion for all stylish young ladies to wear on their noses enormous spectacles, sometimes two and three inches in diameter. It was supposed to give them a lofty and earnest appearance, such as suits the ideal of the haughty Spaniard. In time our eyeglasses will appear quite as absurd as these huge spectacles do now.

When the sight is weak, but with no special disease present, it may be very much improved by one of the following methods: Take a handful of fresh red-peppers, or ginger-root, and pour over them a half pint of pure alcohol. Wipe twice daily the brow above the eye and the temple with a little of this on a soft sponge, and let it dry. Or take a heaping tablespoonful of clean rock salt, and let it dissolve in a quart of rain water. Immerse the face in this every morning, and open the eyes while under the water so that the salt can act directly on the organ. This latter is most excellent also in cases of redness or slight inflammation of the eyes.

When there is a tendency to become near-sighted, it can be prevented by closing the eyes and passing the fingers with a gentle equable pressure from the corner next the nose outward. This should be repeated a number of times every day, and the eye should always be wiped in the same direction. The cornea is thus flattened, and the angle of vision lengthened.

The reverse of this procedure will be found very efficacious when the sight begins to fail from years or over-work. Then the pressure should be made from the outer angles inward. By doing this regularly and skilfully, elderly people can remain gloriously independent of spectacles to any age they are likely to reach.

There are a vast number of diseases of the eye, to most of which we shall make no reference whatever. It should be a rule with every one to have first-class medical advice whenever any trouble, no matter how insignificant, arises in this important and delicate organ. Sometimes the delay of a few hours renders the case hopeless.

Some peculiarly disfiguring disorders, as coming within our special department, must be mentioned. One is "cross-eyes," or "squinting," the *strabismus* of medical men. Every one knows what this is, and every one can imagine how painful it is to a person thus to be singled out as an object of curiosity, and often of ridicule. Moreover, the sight is certain to be impaired sooner or later. Whether both or one eye is affected, the only cure is to have an operation performed, which can be done safely, expeditiously, and with almost certain success.

Another is the loss of the eye from whatever cause. In these cases vision of course can never be restored, but the deformity can be admirably concealed by the adjustment of an artificial eye, made of glass, colored to resemble accurately the remaining eye. There are many little precautions about the use of such an instrument, which the reader can learn from her physician, but which we trust she will never have need to know.

Much more to the purpose is it for us to divulge a few secrets about the brightness and the expression of the eyes. We could disclose some cunning devices in vogue among the fashionable belles of the Old World to give expression to these organs. But these are naughty and dangerous devices, not proper for the women of America to practise. For instance, these reckless belles place a single drop of that deadly poison, prussic acid (dilute, *acid. hydrocyan. dil.* U. S. P.), in the bottom of a wineglass, and hold the glass against the eye for two or three seconds. Or, still more rashly, they take ever so small a quantity, a piece not larger than a grain of rice, of an ointment containing that mortal drug atropia, and this they rub on the brow. The first of these proceedings gives clearness and brilliancy, the second expands the pupil and imparts a fascinating fulness and mellowness to the eye.

Or, again, they take—

But no! our conscience checks us, and we are not going to reveal any more such injurious arts. For injurious they are, as well as dangerous, resulting certainly, if used too often, in impairment of the vision. Let them be left, therefore, to those who make a living by their charms, to actresses, and the belles of the boulevards.

We have known some ladies before going to a ball swallow a teaspoonful of ether (*æther sulphuricus*, U. S. P.). This is a powerful nervous stimulant, and causes the eye to glitter and sparkle, but it, too, is not to be recommended.

Certain slightly pungent and volatile perfumes, such as the oil of thyme and the oil of bitter almonds (which contains prussic acid), are occasionally worn on the handkerchief in order to produce a similar effect. But a healthy eye needs no such aids, and a diseased one is better without them.

A wiser course to improve the expression is by avoiding unseemly habits, such as winking, opening widely the lids, and so forth, and by studying, before a mirror if need be, the management of the ocular muscles. In society, avoid either staring fixedly at a person, looking around constantly, or shunning to meet another's gaze. Allow the eye to lighten up with sympathy, interest, or intelligence, but do not let it roll, or vibrate, or turn upward to show the white below the pupil. It will be pleasing to note how soon moderate daily practice, and a rigid self-control over this organ, will improve and beautify the whole face.

THE EAR AND THE SENSE OF HEARING.

THE FORM AND CARE OF THE EAR.

IN a horse, an ass, or a dog, we naturally look to the ear as the most expressive feature of the animal. It is less significant in man, but still has more influence on the appearance than we usually attribute to it. While it should be distinctly visible from in front, it should not project from the head, and in its form it should present agreeable curves, and not be angular or pointed.

Thorough cleanliness is the most important rule regarding it. Too often in hasty toilettes this is overlooked. The wax should be removed twice a week with a *cure-oreille*, or ear pick, of ivory, steel, or tortoise shell, but care should be had not to employ the least violence. If the wax is hardened, warm water containing a few drops of sulphuric ether should be injected with an ear syringe at night.

A growth of bristly hairs in the ears is very disfiguring. They should be removed in the mode to be described in the chapter on hair. By this means they are eradicated and without pain.

When, as occasionally happens, a spider or other insect enters the ear, there is no occasion for alarm, and no efforts whatever should be made to extract it. The treatment is to fill the ear at once with sweet oil, which is at hand in every house. This destroys the intruder, and the extraction must be left to the physician, as there is great danger to the delicate internal organs of hearing from rough handling.

Some persons have a habit of wearing cotton in their ears to protect them against earache. This is objectionable for many reasons. It dulls the hearing, alters the secretion of wax, changes the expression of the organ, and gives a sickly look.

When the ear obstinately insists on standing out from the head in grown persons, it is next to impossible to prevent it. In children, it is much easier, and therefore every mother should see to it that the children's caps, their bonnet strings, and the folds of the hair, do not impress this unsightly direction on the cartilage. Moreover, it becomes in this respect the duty of parents to forbid school teachers from pulling, boxing, or twisting the ears of their scholars, as is a custom in many schools. Such violence often imprints a permanent unseemly shape, which is the source of much secret mental pain in after years.

The color of the ear should be as light as that of the surrounding flesh, or verge slightly on the pink. But it is not uncommon to see ears with a constant redness, very inconsistent with the demands of cosmetic art. Sometimes this arises from injuries, such as frequent pinching or pulling, more frequently it is the unpleasant memento of some sleigh ride or other exposure to the cold. The tips of the ear are readily frost-bitten, and then acquire this heightened, unhealthy hue. It may be concealed by dusting with French chalk, but it is better to remedy it by washing the parts evening and morning with a lotion made by dissolving a teaspoonful of alum and a teaspoonful of borax in half a pint of rose-water, and two tablespoonfuls of tincture of benzoin.

Injuries not unfrequently mar the symmetry of the ear, and there are various malformations to which it is subject. Most of these can be partly or quite restored by the resources of cosmetic surgery, and no one should hesitate to seek such assistance. It is not worth while to detail at length what these various malformations are, as they are only too readily recognized. Even when the ear is in part or altogether absent, the case is not desperate. An "artificial ear" can be made of vulcanized rubber, or other material, tinted the color of the flesh, and attached to the side of the head with such deftness that its character will escape every ordinary eye. In all cases where there

9

is any defect in the form, color, or position of the ear, it behooves a person to study with especial care the arrangement of the hair best suited to conceal that misfortune.

PIERCING THE EAR, AND EARRINGS.

In England the custom of wearing earrings or pendants has fallen considerably into disuse in the best circles during the last ten years, but with us the large majority of young ladies adhere to it. The operation of piercing the ears which they undergo is too often left to the jeweller or some friend to perform. The result is that it is nothing very uncommon to find it productive of troublesome consequences. A learned professor of surgery states, in a recent work, that he has seen five cases where large and troublesome tumors in the lobe of the ear were caused in this way, and we could easily quote more than one instance recorded in medical literature where even death resulted.

It is wiser, therefore, to have it performed by a medical man, who will take into account the constitution of the girl, the state of her health, and the season of the year, so as to avoid every possible danger. He will also complete it almost without pain by means of some apparatus for suspending sensation in the part.

The proper procedure is to mark the exact spot with a pen, choosing it near the middle of the lobe.

Having then subjected the part for a few seconds to the spray of ether, which renders it insensible. a cork is placed behind to form a firm support. and the aperture made by a three-cornered steel punch. A silver or gold wire is then inserted and left for two or three days, when it is carefully oiled and moved. In a week the canal is usually healed.

No base metal should ever be worn in the ears, and no gold less tnan eighteen carats fine, as the substances used in the alloy of lower grades are liable to irritate and inflame the skin. Heavy rings should not be worn by girls, as the lobes are quite elastic, and may stretch out of all proportion. When from violence the lobe of the ear is torn, or when the aperture for the ring becomes inordinately large, a simple and quickly-performed operation will restore the member to its natural shape. The edges are pared, and by being held in contact soon grow together.

THE NOSE, AND SENSE OF SMELL.

PROPER FORM AND CARE OF THE NOSE.

THE discussion whether a Grecian or straight, or a
Roman or aquiline nose, or any other particular
variety, is the most becoming, is idle, and does not
interest us. The important point is that the organ be
symmetrical, and in harmony with the other features.

The national names we have just mentioned show
how strongly this member characterizes tribes and
families of our race. We all know the thick, prominent, curved, Jewish nose, and do not admire it very
much. No doubt, however, Solomon did, and thought
that the more of it the better, for we find him, in his
"Song of Songs," enumerating in the catalogue of the
beauties of his love, that "thy nose is as the tower of
Lebanon, which looketh toward Damascus," which,
only in an extremely figurative sense indeed, would
be accepted as a compliment by one of our American
fair ones.

(100)

So far have we departed from this ancient ideal, that an unusually prominent nose is often a source of great mortification. It may even have more serious results. The wild and witty French author, Cyrano de Bergerac, was distinguished by a nose which almost deserved to be called a proboscis. Like most others similarly gifted, he was extremely sensitive on the point, and as he was as daring as a lion and an expert swordsman, it was not prudent to twit him about it. By the time he was thirty-five he had challenged for this cause six antagonists, and left every one of them dead on the field.

The artistic rule based on the Greek sculptures is to have the line of the nose straight or very nearly so, its length one-third of that of the face, and its prominence seen in profile one-third of its length. The septum, or division between the nostrils, must be exactly in the middle line of the face; the openings of the nostrils precisely similar, and horizontal in the profile. A thin and pointed, or a gross and flabby nose, is never handsome.

The pure Roman nose is admirably suited to a "stage face," and usually accompanies an energetic, clear-headed, practical, but somewhat hard and selfish character. The Greek type is more consonant with delicate sensibilities, taste, and refinement, but also uncertainty of purpose and self-indulgence. Such, also, were the respective traits of the nations whose names they bear.

The care of the nose commences with cleanliness. While this is true, frequent wiping, sniffing, blowing, or picking should be avoided, and children especially should be hindered from so doing, as from such habits the organ readily assumes an unsightly shape. If there is much irritation of the nostrils, it is a sure sign of some internal disorder, and the physician's opinion should be taken. So, too, the discharge is never excessive in perfect health, and, when it becomes so, it is either owing to worms, dyspepsia, chronic catarrh, or some more serious disorder. Those who are subject to frequent "colds in the head" will infallibly destroy the contour of this prominent feature, and they should remove the tendency at once. This can always be done either by cold ablutions without and within the nostrils, correction of dyspeptic troubles (gastric catarrh), medicated inhalations, the nasal douche, or, lastly, change of climate.

Still more essential is it that the discharge from the nostril should be *odorless*. It must be called a most serious misfortune when this is not the case. The sufferer is offensive to herself, and to every one who approaches her. Her condition demands our most active and sympathizing attention. Often some local irritation produces it, often some constitutional change is taking place, and often that obstinate disease "ozæna," one of the most repulsive we have to deal with, has to be encountered. Within a few months we have been consulted in several cases of the latter complaint in young ladies, whose lives it rendered miserable. Fortunately, if taken early enough in the disease to apply those remedies which medical art provides, it is curable; but it is of the utmost importance to allow no delay in obtaining proper aid.

The dirty habit of snuff-taking leads to various disorders and deformities of the nose, but as we do not ever remember to have seen an American lady cherishing this one of the many little foxes that spoil the vine of beauty, we presume it is unnecessary to detail its ugly assaults.

"Foreign bodies," as surgeons call them, meaning anything that has no business there, are frequently put up the nose by children, or thoughtless persons. They must be extracted very gently, as violence may lacerate the skin or injure the bone, causing lasting disfigurement.

Nature, who is ever careful to protect her delicate pieces of workmanship, plants for this purpose a number of soft, light-colored hairs just inside the entrance of the nostril, to catch the dust and little irritating particles. Sometimes these grow to an unnecessary length, and present a very unprepossessing appearance. In such case the longest and most bristly should be removed, care being taken not to injure in the least the adjacent bone, which misfortune has been known to occur with very unpleasant results. The ether-spray will render the operation altogether painless, though it is quite bearable without it.

DEFECTS IN THE FORM AND COLOR OF THE NOSE.

A person with an ugly nose has much to bear. They must either suffer in silence, or, like Cyrano de Bergerac, whose story we have told, fight many a battle in its defence. We modestly come as consolers to all such. Their cases are not desperate, at any rate not always so.

Some of them have noses leaning more to one side than the other, not placed in the median line of the face. This, to a slight degree, is very common and often hardly noticed, except as it mars the "*tout ensemble*" of the face. In others, again, it is intolerable. Mr. Heather Bigg, of London, who has quite a reputation for treating disfigurements, tells of a young barrister whose nose was so much on one side of his face that it threatened to spoil his prospects at the bar. He applied for relief to Mr. Bigg, who contrived an instrument which forced it by a spring to its proper place. This was worn constantly at night, and occasionally during the day. The success was complete. Similar mechanical appliances should be worn by every one who would rid themselves of this disagreeable obliquity. They must be made and adjusted very carefully to suit each separate case. In young persons they are always successful, but with advancing age the results grow less satisfactory.

A common cause of this crookedness is that persons wipe or blow the nose always with one hand, and pull it frequently, therefore, in one direction. By reversing the direction the trouble is lessened.

Dr. Cid, an inventive surgeon of Paris, noticed that elderly people, who for a long time have worn eye-glasses supported on the nose by a spring, are apt to have this organ long and thin. This he attributes to the compression which the spring exerts on the arteries by which the nose is nourished. The idea occurred to him that the hint could be made useful. Not long afterwards a young lady of fifteen years consulted him, to see if he could restore to moderate dimensions her nose, which was large, fleshy, and unsightly. The trait, he found, was hereditary in her family, as her mother and sister were similarly afflicted. This was discouraging, as hereditary peculiarities are particularly obstinate, but the doctor determined to try his method. He took exact measurements, and had constructed for her a "*lunette pince-nez*," a spring and pad for compressing the artery, which she wore at night, and whenever she conveniently could in the day-time. In three weeks a consolatory diminution was evident, and in three months the young lady was quite satisfied with the improvement in her features. Patience on the one part, and skill on the other, had won the battle. This was more than twenty years ago, and since then the surgeons who have given attention to the subject have had many similar successes.

Speaking of eye-glasses, we may remark that when long used they have another unsightly effect. At the points where they press on the sides of the nose not unfrequently the skin thickens, and forms a callus or warty excrescence. This should be avoided by altering the spot where they are worn, or by having them padded.

A singular and repulsive deformity is occasionally produced by the growth of small pendent tumors, called polypi. inside the nostrils. They are not visible externally. but can be seen within on close examination. They interfere with the voice, rendering it hoarse and nasal; the sufferer cannot breathe freely through the nostrils, and when large they change the face in a manner at once sad and ludicrous, giving it an expression like that of a frog. These tumors used formerly to be seized and torn out by means of a forceps, a painful, bloody, and risky operation. Lately, however, an admirable apparatus has been invented, by which they are surrounded with a wire, and removed instantly and painlessly by a charge of galvano-electricity along the wire.

Blows, falls, and similar injuries sometimes mar the contour of the nose in a shocking manner. They should in all cases be attended to with promptness and skill. Even if neglected, much can be done by an ingenious surgeon in restoration and improvement. A nose that is too flat can be raised, one with unequal apertures can be modified, one too thin can be expanded. Cosmetic surgery is rich in devices here, all of which are very available in children and young persons, less so when years have hardened and stiffened the cartilages and bones.

Even when there is no nose at all, cosmetic surgery does not quit the field. Quite the contrary. Here is one of its most brilliant victories. For, what think you? it is ready to furnish a nose, not of silver or gutta-percha, though it can do this too, but one "out of whole cloth," a good, living, fleshly nose. It will transplant you one from the arm, or the forehead, Romanic or Grecian, *à volonté;* it will graft it adroitly into the middle of the face, with two regular nostrils, and a handsome bridge; and it will almost challenge nature herself to improve on the model.

The surgeon, in this triumphant operation, takes advantage of a strange property of parts of our body to continue growing when they are transplanted. To give an example: At German universities there is a great passion for duels. It is an exciting pastime, and it is not very dangerous. The opponents are perfectly protected everywhere but in the face, and the weapons they use are swords very sharp at the points. They never thrust but swing them, so that the worst wound is usually a clean and shallow cut. Once we knew or a valorous student who had the end of his nose cleanly taken off by a sweep of his opponent's weapon. The fragment was at once picked up, dusted, and fastened where it belonged with a piece of sticking plaster. In a week's time you would hardly have guessed that it had ever been off.

But a French surgeon tells a more wonderful experience. He transplanted the tail of one rat to the middle of the back of another. The tail continued to grow, and was as healthy as ever! Truly, it must have had a strong dose of the vital principle.

All this is very significant, and pertinent to our theme; for it shows us how sanguine we may be in hoping to replace members which have been lopped off or injured.

What we have to say about red noses, and so forth, we shall defer for the chapter on the skin and complexion, where it properly belongs.

THE SENSE OF SMELL, AND PERFUMERY.

There is so much to be said about the sense of smell and odors, bad and good, that it is difficult to know where to begin—still more difficult to know where to stop. We have a friend who is an enthusiast on the topic. Sometimes he will button-hole us, and

ignoring all our polite little attempts at escape, treat
us to an extempore lecture on his hobby.

" The sense of smell," he begins, " is beyond all com-
parison the most delicate, ethereal, and noble of all
the senses. You can put a grain of pure musk in a
room for years, have your windows open, occupy it
daily, but every person who enters will at once detect
the perfume, and leave the apartment carrying with
him some slight particle of musk. At the end of ten
years, weigh your musk, and you will find the full grain,
not diminished by the hundredth fraction of a milli-
gramme. Can you see, feel, hear, taste these infinitely
little molecules? No! you can only smell them.
Mark the lower animals. Does the dog trust to eye
or ear to recognize his master? No! to his scent
alone.

"You doctors give your medicines by the stomach
or the skin. If I were a doctor and had a diploma, I
should found a new school. I would give my medicines by the nose. You smile. But I can prove to
you that organic matter has ten-thousand-fold more
influence when thus administered, than in any other
way. I have a brother, a sturdy, sun-browned farmer,
to whom the odor of his new-mown hay. to you so
delicious, is a poison. It throws him into fits of sten-
torian sneezings, he chokes and gasps as if he would
strangle. The doctors call it 'hay-asthma,' or 'rose
cold.' and pour annually down his throat quarts of

drugs, without a shadow of benefit. Of course not. Why don't they apply the remedies to the part affected? If he had a sore toe they would not bandage his finger. They should cure him by odors.

"I have a cousin, no nervous invalid but a hardy sailor, who hasn't seen thirty summers, but has ploughed every ocean and trodden every continent on this globe. Bring him into a room where there is a watermelon, and he is at once seized with such paroxysms of sneezing and coughing that he can hardly speak a word. You don't approve of infinitesimals. Do those who believe in them ever divide medicines more minutely, think you, than these odors?"

"Hold!" exclaimed we, goaded by this last thrust from our design to let him talk himself out as quickly as possible, "hold, you don't understand the subject. We will explain it in two words. The Schneiderian membrane when in a condition of hyperæsthesia—"

"Enough," replies our incorrigible friend, "I grant it. At any rate I would rather die in ignorance, than hear an explanation which begins in that manner. Pardon the hit. I thought you looked bored, and I wanted to stir you up to listen to my theory of perfumery as a fine art. The ear has music; the eye its complementary and contrasted colors; so there is a music to the sense of smell, a sweet accord of odors, as fixed, as much under law, as the sonatas of Beethoven. In some riper civilization we shall have operas of

fragrant scents, and the enamored lover shall no longer
bring on his head the maledictions of the neighbors for
making night hideous with his guitar and hoarse voice,
but shall waft to his lady-love a voiceless serenade of
distilled essences from the bowers of love."

"My dear sir," we broke in. "this is really too absurd. Besides, pardon us for looking at our watch,
but we have a case of leg at the hospital——"

"Absurd," said he in some heat, entirely disregard-
ing our last clause—"Look here! do you see this work
by a learned German professor of Leipzig? What can
you say to that?"

And drawing a small volume from his pocket, he
showed us what at first we supposed was a series of
musical notes, but in fact was the harmonic scale of
perfumes, arranged in different keys and accords, with
a series of comments by the author, explaining the
necessity of mingling essential oils according to these
laws in order to form new perfumes, and to affect
pleasantly the olfactory sense. We looked at the
title-page and saw: "Toilletten-chemie, von Dr. Heinrich
Hirzel, Professor a. d. Universität zu Leipzig, 1866."

In truth our friend has some foundation for his
speculations. The proper use of perfumes, quite as
much as their manufacture, demands an acquaintance
with their accords.

In the first place, his hint of the unpleasant effects
of certain odors on some people should be borne in

mind. The animal perfumes, musk, civet, and amber-
gris, as well as camphor, new-mown hay, and patchoulis, are extremely disagreeable to many. We
know a lady who cannot smell musk without it giving
her a headache. Moreover, bergamot, patchoulis, and
musk are in our large American cities especially
popular among the lower and the immoral classes of
women, which is reason enough why they should be
avoided by a lady. No powerful or pungent scents
should be used, as they lead to a suspicion that they
are employed to conceal some bad smell natural to
the person. Rare old Ben Jonson, in his drama of
" The Silent Woman," has one of his characters say:—

> " Still to be powd'red, still perfumed,
> Lady, it is to be presumed,
> Though art's hid causes are not found,
> All is not sweet, all is not sound."

It is well at times to appear without any artificial
odor whatever, with only the subtle, fresh, and rich
aroma of perfect health and cleanliness, that indescri-
bable *odeur de jolie femme*, as Alexandre Dumas, *fils*,
calls it in one of his novels. There is another reason
for the same occasional deprivation. The nerves of
smell soon lose their fine sensibility, or else acquire an
unhealthy irritability, if long subjected to the same
stimulus. The wine-bibber is never a connoisseur in
vintages, the *gourmand* is never a *gourmet*, and the

person forever smelling strong perfumes rarely can use them judiciously.

Therefore, one should avoid wearing constantly a favorite perfume. Change it rather for one of the same accord. For example, sandal-wood, which in an impalpable powder is now sold at our Japanese stores, accords well with rose-geranium, acacia blossoms, orange flowers, or camphor; musk suits with rose, tuberose, tonka bean, or jonquille; and so forth. Such a discrimination will be as readily made by a naturally keen or well-educated nose, as a tune will be caught by a cultivated ear; and a discord will be as promptly detected by the one sense as by the other.

But the subject is so extensive, and furthermore as it does not actually lie within our present subject, we must leave it. Should our friends wish for a full discussion of the topic, we must some time start our enthusiastic acquaintance on his favorite branch, and retail for their benefit what he tells us. Or we shall urge him to address himself directly to them, and thus make a double escape for ourselves.

So far as relates to the correction of unpleasant odors about the person, we shall not omit to give full directions about those when we come to speak of the skin, breath, etc.

10*

THE MOUTH, LIPS, TEETH, AND BREATH.

THE MOUTH AND LIPS.

THE home of smiles and merry laughter, the spot where love seals its vows, and friendship offers its warmest pledges, whence winged words bring to us, like carrier pigeons, the thoughts of other souls, the mouth next comes before us for study. Its parts and outlines must be in keeping with each other and with the remaining members of the face. Here, more distinctly than in any other feature, does a debased ancestry leave a vicious imprint, and a countenance please or displease us. More than one woman lives in history by her mouth.

There, for example, is Margaret Maultasche, Margaret the Pouch mouth, " rugged dragoon major of a woman," as Carlyle calls her, conspicuous enough in her day and generation, now five hundred years agone, not only by her thick lips and big mouth, but by her huge possessions in Austria, and the knack she had for

keeping them in those troublesome times. She is sure
to be remembered "when your Pompadour, Duchess
of Cleveland, of Kendal, and other high-rouged, unfortunate females, whom it is not proper to speak of
without necessity, shall have sunk beneath the Histori-
cal." Let us hope so, for with all her ruggedness she
was true wife and of sterling metal, and worth more
than the whole crowd of the others.

The mouth should be of moderate size, the corners
symmetrical, when closed the line perfectly horizontal,
the lips well defined and rosy red, the lower slightly
more prominent than the upper, both covering readily
the teeth but not redundant. The crowning charm of
a pretty mouth are wreathed smiles.

> " Such as hang on Hebe's cheek,
>   And love to live in dimple sleek ;"

or, lest we put the mark discouragingly high, such as
may wreathe almost any face, if the owner will take
care to cultivate it. How many there are whom mirth
robs of half their good looks! It often demands
practice before the mirror in order to correct one's self
of ungracious *tics*, which mar the pleasure we would
otherwise give by a smile. The lips should part moderately, disclosing the teeth, but not the gums, and not
contorting the rest of the visage, while yet the whole
face sympathizes in the mirthfulness.

It is anything but pleasing to see a grin without
gladness. The ancients called such a grimace the

Sardonic laugh, because it was supposed to be produced by eating the poisonous herb sardonica. Some persons rather affect it. Dickens, in one of his novels, speaks of a character whose nearest approach to gayety was to have his moustache move up and his nose come down, and when the *blasé* style is in vogue, a vacant grin is the nearest approach to a smile permissible.

For cosmetic reasons, immoderate laughter is objectionable. It keeps the muscles on the stretch, destroys the contour of the features, and produces wrinkles. It is better to cultivate a " classic repose."

Still more decidedly should the habit of " making mouths" be condemned, whether it occur in conversing in private, or to express emotions. It never adds to the emphasis of the discourse, never improves the looks, and leads to actual malformations.

Children sometimes learn to suck and bite their lips. This distorts these organs, and unless they are persuaded to give it up betimes a permanent deformity will arise.

When the lips have once assumed a given form, it is difficult to change them. Those that are too thin can occasionally be increased by adopting the plan of sucking them. This forces a large quantity of blood to the part, and consequently a greater amount of nutriment. When too large, compresses can sometimes, but not always, be used to effect. We have employed silver plates connected by a wire spring, or a mould of stiff leather. Either may be worn at night, or in the house during the day.

Such a malformation is often peculiar to some races and families. Negroes notoriously have their thick, coarse lips as a trait of race. The Hapsburgs, the royal house of Austria, are distinguished by a hanging nether lip. They have always been an ill-favored family, and though they have managed to marry rich heiresses, and absorb quantities of land, their homeliness has been in their way. Albert I, son of Rudolf of Hapsburg, founder of the line, an ugly, loose-lipped man, blind of an eye, was rejected as Emperor by Pope Boniface on account of his looks. "What!" said the Pope, "that one-eyed, clownish, thick-lipped fellow? he is not fit to be Emperor." But Albert killed with his own hand his rival for the imperial purple, and did become Emperor in spite of his big lips, the Pope, and the whole set of them.

Girls who have a scrofulous tendency in their constitutions are liable to an excessive growth of their upper lip. It becomes hard, puffed out, and twice as thick as natural. The veins are large, but there is little or no pain. This is an obstinate complaint, but it can be cured if a skilful surgeon is consulted in time.

We have seen not a few unfortunate people who, when they smile or laugh, turn the upper lip almost inside out, and show a fold or crease of the red, mucous membrane which lines it. This is a most disagreeable spectacle, fatal to comeliness. It can, and it should be, cured. An operation is necessary, but only a slight and not very painful one, or it can be rendered entirely painless by ether.

If tumors and local swellings appear on the lips, they should be promptly submitted to a medical adviser, as they can only be successfully treated by the more recondite arts of medicine.

A deformity of birth only too common is that familiarly known as "hare-lip," so called because the upper lip is cleft or divided by a fissure, like that of hares or rabbits. This not only gives a hideous expression to the features, but frequently interferes with the pronunciation of words. It can be very neatly remedied by a surgeon, and no one should hesitate to undergo the necessary operation. In children it is best to have it remedied either just before or after they have their first teeth; that is, either when they are five or six months, or between two and three years of age.

Coral lips, cherry lips, rosy lips, such as those of beauteous Queen Guinevere:—

> " A man had given all other bliss,
> And all his worldly worth for this,
> To waste his whole heart in one kiss
> Upon her perfect lips,"

have inspired many a poet with immortal songs. But there is many a fair one whose lips are neither coralline nor roseate, but pale and faded, or puffed and purple.

The latter depends often on serious disease. We see it in consumption, and in certain disorders of the heart. It should be regarded with anxiety, and means adopted to restore the general health.

Pale lips betoken general feebleness of circulation. They are very common in young girls inclined to chlorosis or green-sickness. Generally, a judicious course of tonics with bathing and exercise will remedy them. Some girls bite and suck their lips in order to make them red. It is a foolish habit, which may injure their shape. No coloring matter should be put on the lips, as it may be too readily swallowed. But if persons will employ something, then the least injurious is the *rouge en feuilles*, of Monin of Paris. A soft, moist, woollen cloth is pressed on the paper, and then passed gently over the lips. This gives them a rosy tint, which is tolerably durable and very natural. What cautions are necessary in using rouge, and which are the best preparations, we shall discuss in full when we treat of the skin.

Dryness, brownness, and cracking of the lips, when obstinate, usually depend on some disorder of the stomach or internal organs. We were recently consulted on this account, by a lady who had tried in vain sundry "lip-salves," which her druggist had in his shop. On inquiry, we found she was suffering from one of those numerous complaints peculiar to her sex. We treated her for this, and when it was remedied, the trouble with the lips passed away under the use of simple glycerine. So important is it, in even the most trifling blemishes of the face, to investigate the workings of the whole system!

Nearly all the lip-salves sold under whatever high-sounding names and in whatever elegance of wrappings, are of spermaceti ointment, colored, perfumed, sweetened, and occasionally with the addition of a small quantity of alum or borax, and of glycerine. The last-mentioned substance in the form of " glycerine cream," that is, well beaten with lard, or with castor oil, and scented, is an excellent application, provided the glycerine is chemically pure, which, we regret to say, is rarely the case. Persons prone to irritations of the lips should provide themselves a supply of some such salve from a first-class druggist, and use a little every night and morning during the winter. Bathing the lips, before applying it, in water in which some alum or borax has been dissolved (a teaspoon even full to a tumbler of water) will be found of great service.

An unsightly spot occasionally forms at the corners of the mouth, moist and reddish, with a tendency to crust over and be tender. This arises usually from acidity of the saliva, and is connected with indigestion and " heart-burn." It can be temporarily helped, and sometimes cured, by rinsing the mouth several times a day with a solution of bicarbonate of soda, (teaspoonful to a pint of water), and anointing the spot with this preparation :—

Oxide of zinc	80 grains;
Spermaceti ointment	half an ounce ;
Otto of roses	a drop.

When this does not give satisfaction after a week's trial, a physician should be consulted, in order that the digestive functions be looked after.

" Fever-blisters" is the popular name given to an eruption on the lips, very troublesome to some persons, arising from a cold, a slight feverish attack, or an irregular or excessive meal. It commences as a hard, hot, painful lump on the lip, and soon changes into a vesicle or blister. In a week or ten days it disappears, leaving for a while a red spot But this is too long a time to remain disfigured, if there is any help for it. There *is* help in various ways. In the first place, the sore spot should never be rubbed or scratched. At the very outset, it should be cautiously touched with this preparation every few hours :—

Carbolic acid	ten drops;
Glycerine	a teaspoonful;
Otto of roses	two drops.

If this does not check it, the little blisters should be moistened with a solution of one grain of permanganate of potash in a tablespoonful of rose-water, and not wiped, but dusted with fine starch, or French chalk (which is better). This shortens the duration of the

11

complaint, and prevents the red mark from remaining so long as it otherwise would.

Sores of any kind about the lips are almost as disagreeable to one's companions as to one's self. The perfumed oxide of zinc ointment mentioned above will be found of real value in most of them. The lower lip is a favorite seat of one of the varieties of cancer, and then must either be treated by subcutaneous injections, with which we have witnessed at least one most admirable cure ; or else the lip has to be removed by the knife. The former method should always be tried first, as in case of success the face is much less disfigured.

While upon this subject we wish to impress upon our readers the imprudence and dangers they run in using cups, tumblers, towels, or anything which others have used, without a thorough washing. Diseases of the most disgusting and frightful character have been often contracted by so doing. Nor should they ever allow themselves to be kissed by acquaintances in whom they have not the fullest confidence. There is related in a recent medical periodical, the story of a young lady of Pennsylvania, who, from the innocent kiss of a young gentleman at a picnic, became the victim of the most hideous disease, perhaps, known to medicine. Let her case be a warning to all others to reserve this favor for the dearest and the most worthy only.

THE TEETH.

What beauty is there in a smile, unless it discloses two symmetrical rows of

> "Delicate, little, pearl-white wedges,
> All transparent at the edges ?"

There is no excuse in our day, when dental surgery is practised with such signal success, for marring the pleasure of the beholder by their absence. Bad teeth do worse than this. They cause foul breath, they give rise to wrinkles and falling in of the cheeks, they excite atrocious neuralgias, they disturb the digestion, disorder the sight, and not unfrequently deprave the whole system. It is the first precept of health and beauty to put them in the best order, and to keep them so.

This branch of cosmetic medicine has been so thoroughly studied, and is exclusively practised by such scientific and capable men in all our large cities, that we shall say nothing about the means adopted to repair, or to extract, or to manufacture, or to allay pain in teeth, but confine ourselves wholly to their preservation.

To begin at the beginning, the child during teething should be surrounded by those precautions with regard to diet, etc., which pertain to the hygiene of infancy, and which need not be rehearsed here. The permanent teeth commence to appear at the age of seven years, and frequently the latest of them, the "wisdom teeth" as they are called, do not arrive until adult age is reached. During the whole of this time it is highly important to see that none of them grow crooked, irregular, or too close. Judicious pressure, if necessary the extraction of one or two, will certainly restore them to their proper places. Parents should not be in a hurry to draw the "baby teeth." Let them almost or quite fall out by themselves. This insures a well developed base for their permanent successors.

The second teeth should be thirty-two in number, symmetrically disposed in the upper and lower jaws, hard, white, and capable of active service. Such a set is almost a sure indication of sound digestion, healthy nutrition, and a good constitution.

A third set sometimes appears in aged persons, and are in every respect as sound and useful as their previous ones. But when people reach fourscore, they have not much to do with cosmetic medicine, nor it with them, so we shall not delay ourselves with these extraordinary cases.

The first rule about teeth is the simplest: *use them.* They were given us to chew our food, and unless we put them to this use in earnest, they will give out for want of something to do, and the stomach will give out from having too much to do. Chew, therefore, the food thoroughly, and chew on both sides, not at once, like Sancho Panza, but alternately, so that all can have a fair share of labor. The tooth is like the arm; use it regularly, and it will be healthy, well-developed, handsome; give it little or nothing to do, and it becomes weak, soft, unsightly.

This is all the advantage (for the teeth) there is in "whole-meal bread," bran bread, and so forth, which of late years have been much preached about. There is no necessity for such unusual diet. In the army it was remarked how well the men's teeth were preserved. A dentist of acknowledged skill has told us he saw this in many instances, and attributes it to the "hard tack," the dry, tough soldier-crackers the men ate. They were forced to chew them thoroughly, and thus their teeth had more to do, and were the better for it.

There is no need of "hard tack," either. Simply masticate deliberately and well such food as is set before you, and the result will be the same.

But looking at this sentence again, we are constrained to modify it. Food may be, doubtless daily is, set before you which, so far as your teeth are concerned, you will do wisely to decline, or to partake of but sparingly. Any food or drink very hot or cold injures the enamel. This "enamel" is the external, white, glittering part of the tooth. It is chiefly lime, and anything sour corrodes or softens the lime, to the injury and final destruction of the whole tooth. Therefore, acid fruits, drinks, or dressings are hurtful, if taken constantly.

There is much discussion whether sugar, sugar candy, confectionery, and similar "goodies," ought to be renounced. We think a moderate indulgence in pure sugar and well-made confections entirely harmless. The sugar changes to an acid in the mouth if retained there, so that the habit of keeping candy long between the teeth, or eating it very constantly, has its dangers. Then some confections, such as sour-drops, tamarinds, and others, are acidulated by a little tartaric or weak sulphuric acid, which is seriously and immediately hurtful. Clean cane sugar and maple sugar are used in extraordinary quantities where they are produced, and they .o not corrode the teeth at all. So let the chil ben keep their mintsticks, and don't debar them from the sugar-plums. It is possible they may live long, and find few pleasures at once more enjoyable and more innocent.

"Use as not abusing," is the rule. Teeth were never meant for nut-crackers, nor for scissors to cut thread, as so many women seem to think while sewing, nor for a rack to hold scissors, pins, and needles, nor for a corkscrew to pull a cork from a bottle, nor for pincers or a vice to hold a piece of muslin, nor for any of a hundred purposes to which they are daily put.

"But I have used them thus for years, and it has not hurt them at all."

Indeed. "The pitcher that goes oft to the well,"—
do you know the proverb? It is somewhat musty.

There is another abuse of the teeth, the mouth, and
the whole body, which we may as well delicately repre-
hend. We mean—well, not to put too fine a point
upon it, as the immortal Micawber says—"snuff-dipping." It is foolish to deny that in certain parts of
our country this disgusting habit prevails widely
among the better classes of society, and is nigh universal among the lower. We passed several days,
once, in the house of a lady by birth, wealth, and position, the wife of a General of some distinction (Fede-
ral or Confederate we say not), whom we saw using
with caution, but with assiduity, the hateful dipping-
stick. A leading snuff manufacturer tells us that his
market is chiefly for this purpose, and that certain
brands are notoriously used in no other way. Now,
there is nothing which ever has, or ever can be said
against smoking or chewing, from King James' "Coun-
terblast against Tobacco" downward, which does not
apply with tenfold force to this nauseous indulgence.

We are no tobacco-phobes. We confess, indeed, to
having gazed without repugnance, even with sentiments
akin to admiration, at some dark-eyed Spanish damsel,
delicately applying to her ripe lips the fragrant ciga-
rette, and wreathing her raven tresses in odorous cir-
clets of silvery clouds. But snuff-dipping, pah! The
offence is rank. Let us leave it.

The particles of food which remain between the teeth soon ferment, and become injurious to the enamel. Therefore, after every meal the mouth should be well rinsed with water, as near the natural temperature of the body as may be. Next, a toothpick should be employed to extract whatever fragments have not been removed. The best toothpicks are of quill, tortoise-shell, ivory, or gold. No other materials, neither wood nor base metals, should be chosen.

The toothpick is an instrument of the toilet much less employed by ladies in this country than in Europe, and than it deserves to be. In Germany, vases of them are placed on the dinner-table with as much regularity as the saltcellar. It is related of Prince von Kaunitz, Prime Minister of Maria Theresa of Austria, and greatest fop and diplomatist of his day, that in this respect he was so finical that whenever he went out to dine, he had his servant bring a box containing all sorts and shapes of toothpicks. These he would use between the courses. One day, a guest, who disliked the supercilious old nobleman, cried out to a servant, "Waiter, bring the Prince von Kaunitz some towels and water. He forgot to make his toilet before coming." After that, the Prince never accepted an invitation to dine out, even with the Empress. Poor man! He was so afraid of death that he would never permit the word to be mentioned in his presence. By devoting himself to his health, he lived beyond fourscore, and then, out of pique at some slight from the court, starved himself to death!

When the gums are tender, or the teeth show a tendency to decay, or the breath is fetid, a mouth-wash should be used several times a day, and on retiring. The best of these are spirits of camphor, half a teaspoonful in a wineglass of water: the same amount of honey-of-roses (*Mel rosarum*, U. S. P.) to the water: a teaspoonful of pure French brandy, or of a mixture of equal parts of tincture of myrrh and compound tincture of cinchona, in the same quantity of water. The temperature of all washes, and all fluids used in cleansing the mouth, should be near that of the body.

There are certain substances which are used as preservatives of the teeth. The best is wood charcoal, especially that of the areca nut, in an impalpable powder. This nut is brought from Java, and its charcoal in powder is probably the best dentifrice in the world. It sweetens the breath, strengthens and whitens the teeth, removes the tartar, prevents toothache, and gives the gums and lips an attractive red color. Unfortunately, the supply is limited, and nine-tenths of that sold as areca-nut charcoal is made from willow wood. About as much of the charcoal should be used as can be held on the point of a knife. It should be placed in the mouth on retiring at night, and gently rubbed into the interstices of the teeth. In the morning it is to be carefully rinsed out. The only objection to charcoal is, that it occasionally leaves a dark line at the base of the teeth. This can be prevented by attention, and by keeping the mouth closed during sleep —a very important point to observe for all who would have sound teeth and a sweet mouth.

We next come to the choice and the use of the *toothbrush*, a modern invention, though substitutes for it, such as pieces of soft wood, coarse woollen cloth, and so forth, have been familiar adjuncts of the toilette table time out of mind. The Chinese ladies aim to have their teeth black, the Persians red, the Japanese gilt, but we have a preference for the natural white, and how to preserve that pearly lustre without injury to the enamel is one of the problems of the cosmetic artist.

The brush should be used morning and night, not violently but thoroughly, on the front, back, and crowns of all the teeth. The bristles should be soft, not stiff nor harsh, and of unequal length in each tuft, so that they will reach to the interstices of the teeth. They should be cut convexly, so as to adapt them to the inner side of the teeth, and arranged in three or four rows. Such brushes are now manufactured in England, and can be obtained in this city and elsewhere.

There are some objections to the tooth-brush. It is apt to scratch the gums and wear the enamel to an extent which is injurious. Owing to the stiffness of even soft bristles, they do not reach into the inequalities of the teeth, and the sensation they convey to a sensitive mouth is often so disagreeable as to limit their use. We are for these reasons inclined to regard with great favor the recently introduced device of *tooth-sponges.* These are fine sponges, about the size of a large pigeon-egg, mounted firmly on handles of ivory or wood. Some are bleached to snowy whiteness, others soaked in odorous or odontalgic liquids which impart to them salubrious and pleasant qualities.

These tooth-sponges are soft, searching, and pleasant to the most tender gums. They are readily cleansed, carry a dentifrice more neatly than a brush, and seem to have no objectionable qualities.

There is a host of dentifrices, tooth-powders, and tooth tinctures, offered in the market. We advise our readers to be guarded in their use of secret preparations, no matter how loudly and expensively they are advertised, and no matter how pleasant they may seem on use. It is easy to whiten the teeth by the use of acids and corrosive or gritty substances, which will soon destroy them, and it is reasonable to suppose that any dentifrice, which is a secret preparation, may contain ingredients which are dangerous, and dare not be made known. An assertion to the contrary has the less weight, as when a man knowingly sells such injurious stuff, he will not stickle at a falsehood to conceal its noxious qualities.

We shall now give a number of tooth-powders which are harmless, efficient, and agreeable. We have used them in our practice for years, sometimes one, sometimes the other, as persons preferred or seemed to require, for some teeth and gums demand different preparations from others. The best of all is the freshly prepared charcoal of the areca nut, or of willow, in impalpable powder. It should be kept tightly corked, and used without the addition of any other substance.

An excellent ordinary powder, where camphor is not disagreeable, is—

Precipitated chalk	seven drachms ;
Powdered camphor	half a drachm ;
Powdered orris root	one drachm.

Mix them thoroughly.

The following is an admirable paste for occasional use :—

White, dried castile soap, in fine powder,	
Sepia, in powder,	equal parts.

Mix to the consistency of paste with fresh, rectified honey, and add a few drops of oil of teaberry (Gaultheria). It should be used *only* occasionally, as the sepia wears the enamel when often applied.

Another good preparation is—

Sugar of milk	two ounces ;
Tannic acid	quarter of an ounce ;
Red lake	half a drachm ;
Oil of cloves, teaberry, or anise	a few drops.

Mix carefully. This is particularly useful when the teeth have been stained by taking medicines containing iron.

When the gums are sore and spongy with a tendency to bleed, the following should be used:—

Precipitated chalk	one ounce ;
Powdered borax	half an ounce ;
Powdered myrrh	quarter of an ounce ;
Powdered orris-root	quarter of an ounce.

If it is desired to whiten the teeth very rapidly, the following powder may be obtained, but ordinarily it should never be employed more than once or twice a week, as it wears the enamel with great rapidity. Pumice-stone is one of the objectionable ingredients in secret tooth-powders.

Pumice-stone in impalpable powder	one ounce ;
Bicarbonate of soda	half an ounce ;
Powdered talc	half an ounce ;
Some flavoring oil	a few drops.

With the pumice-stone omitted, the remaining articles can be freely used when the saliva is acid and the breath sour.

If one or another of these powders is judiciously applied, and the other precautions for the care of the teeth observed, we can almost guarantee our readers that they will live long without taking a seat in the dentist's chair, unless the mischief has already been done. They must, furthermore, avoid cleansing the teeth with cigar ashes, or causing the gums to bleed with the tooth-pick or brush, or rubbing them with cream of tartar or any other acid. But they may, if they please, in the early summer crush a ripe strawberry around the teeth before retiring, and let the pulp remain there during the night. It is a marvellous secret for giving the enamel a lustrous hue, and the breath a richly fruity aroma, comparable to the zephyr wafted from some Isle of Eden in a summer sea. A lotion of permanganate of potash, which is esteemed very highly in Europe, we shall mention later, when we come to speak of offensive breath, and how to prevent it.

A curious fact in physiology will make an appropriate close to this section. It has, moreover, a direct connection with the beauty of the teeth. Though they have no real circulation, their color is found to change with the changes in the health. In bilious people they become yellow; in scrofulous and consumptive patients they show occasionally an unnaturally pearly and translucent whiteness. It is absurd, therefore, for all to wish to have teeth similar to the most admired models.

THE VOICE.

What a touch of nature is that where Lear, bending with unfathomable sorrow in his aged eyes over Cordelia's body, thinks he hears some half-whispered

word, and lest those around should utter the doubt he
feels himself, says:—

> Her voice was ever soft,
> Gentle and low; an excellent thing in woman !

This is the verdict of every society. A harsh, mas-
culine voice, strident, loud, or shrill, we associate with
fish-wives, with throats rasped by fiery liquors, with
viragos, and common-scolds. It was not with such a
tone, but "in a clear, melodiously-piercing voice," as
the chronicles are particular to say, that the Empress
Maria Theresa appeared, babe in arms, before the
black-bearded Magyars of Hungary, to appeal to them
to save her crown. The proud, semi-barbaric nobles
were touched, overpowered, by the sight and the tone.
They sprang to their feet, swung aloft their naked
swords, and with one voice shouted, *Vitam et san-
guinem pro rege nostro Maria Theresa;* "Our life and
our blood for our King Maria Theresa"—not Queen,
for a queen to rule over Hungary, those haughty
magnates would never brook—in grammar.

A soft, clear, modulated tone of voice should be assiduously cultivated. It is a valuable acquirement in
society to read well, especially poetry. Children
should be trained not merely to pronounce distinctly,
but to express feeling in tone. For this, parlor theatricals are admirably fitted, and have ever been favorite
amusements in polished circles. Our national talent
is much inferior in this respect to that of the Italians

for example. We are hardly equal to their system of private dramas. They fix on the plot, the acts, the scenes, and the incidents, and then, the parts being assigned, leave each participant to fill up the words for himself or herself. Travellers say it is really astonishing with what wit and fluency they acquit themselves.

Some persons are very subject to hoarseness on every exposure, to "a frog in the throat," as it is familiarly called from the croaking sound of the voice. They will find this frequently prevented by bathing the throat night and morning in cold water, or salt and water, by gargling every morning with a weak solution of tannic acid, or alum, and by guarding against varying the protection of the throat. When the hoarseness is already present, it can be often dispersed by inhaling the fumes of iodine, or the steam from hot water poured on chlorate of potash, or by taking slowly the white of an egg, beaten up with sugar. Still more efficient, and a favorite with singers, is a tumbler of water containing five or six drops of dilute nitric acid (*Acidum nitricum dilutum*, U. S. P.) swallowed slowly twice a day. A lemon is often sucked for the same purpose. When the hoarseness is permanent, as it often is in clergymen and other public speakers, the use of the Turkish bath twice a week has a most excellent effect.

The training of the *voice in singing* is a subject of

such importance that we cannot enter upon it here.
Suffice it to say that very useful hints may often be
learned by having the throat examined by the laryn-
goscope, either when there is a difficulty in forming
certain sounds, or where the voice becomes "cracked,"
or "broken." These latter conditions depend generally
on some local debility in the throat, which can be
treated and amended. No singer who values her powers should sing in the open air, or too long at a time,
or on a higher key than is easy for her, or at a period
when her general health is at all below par. We know
an instance where a single infraction of these rules has
ruined completely and irremediably an excellent so-
prano.

Often a course of natural sulphur waters, at one of
the "Sulphur Springs" in Virginia or elsewhere, is of
signal service in restoring and improving the failing
powers of the voice. When shallowness of the purse,
or other reason, prevents one from taking this agreeable prescription, an artificial sulphur water can be
prepared and used at home with good, but not so good
effects.

We can go through the world comfortably without
singing; but we cannot get along at all pleasantly
without the power of distinct speech. It is, therefore,
a most important branch of cosmetic surgery to
remedy defects in the articulation and the pronunciation of letters, syllables, and words, such as lisping,

12*

stuttering, stammering, thickness or indistinctness of the voice, loss of voice, or difficulty in enunciation. Most of these difficulties depend upon remediable causes. But it is singular how completely this branch is neglected by most physicians.

When, for instance, we commence to devote our attention to the methods recommended to cure stammering, we do not find a single author in the English language who treats it from a scientific point of view. It has been left in the hands of elocutionists and charlatans, who are given to lauding some individual method of their own as successful in every case.

Such claims bear upon their face their own refutation. It is as if a man pretended to cure blindness by some one remedy. Blindness arises from a host of diverse conditions of the organ. So does stammering.

It may be the innervation which is at fault, and then electricity promises much. It is sometimes an inborn muscular debility, and then we can employ the instruments devised by Dr. Itard and others, with fair prospects. Occasionally it is owing to a contraction of certain muscles, and these were the cases which the famous surgeon Dieffenbach cured by cutting those muscles. Not unfrequently it is of the nature of chorea, when we must treat it with internal remedies as we do that disease. Frequently, certain letters and sounds only are stammered, and then a series of lingual gymnastics will be followed by prompt amendment. Each case must be carefully examined and treated according to its own nature. If this is done, and if the sufferers will make a most determined resolution to recover, they will do so.

Demosthenes was a stammerer when young. He used to stand for hours on the sea-beach of Attica, and with his mouth full of pebbles, declaim loud enough to drown the roaring of the surf. He cured himself. We have heard of a young gentleman who imitated his example with praiseworthy persistence. He was not in the least benefited. He did not reflect that his stammering had quite a different cause from that of the great Athenian orator.

The letters which are pronounced with difficulty often betray the seat of trouble. If the k sounds like g hard, there is rigidity of muscle present; if the r sounds like an l, the tongue is at fault; if the b, p, or v, is mispronounced, the lips or teeth may be the cause.

The stammerer has no child's play before him, but in the majority of cases he can confidently expect decided amendment or complete restoration, if he is diligent, patient, untiringly vigilant. The cure should not be commenced before the sixteenth or seventeenth year, as self-control is wanting; nor is it favorable after the age of thirty has been passed, as then inveterate habit has grown into nature.

The entire loss of the voice, so that one cannot speak above a whisper, is a common affliction. It is generally a nervous disease, and plays curious freaks. A young lady, for instance, a teacher in one of our public schools, lost her voice daily when school closed, but it always came back to her the next morning when the school opened. Another conversed without difficulty, in her natural voice, from the time she rose in the morning until noon. But as soon as the clock struck twelve, she could not make a sound above a whisper until the next morning. We had under our care a young man, who for seven months had not spoken aloud. We asked him one day to tell the servant to bring some water. Without thinking what he was doing, he called loudly in his natural voice, and had no trouble in using it afterwards.

Herodotus, the Greek historian, tells this story of Crœsus, King of Lydia. Fortune had blessed him with wide lands, untold riches, and an accomplished son, but had withheld from the latter the gift of speech above a whisper. Crœsus called in the wise men and the physicians, and when they failed, finally appealed to the gods themselves. He sent rich gifts to the far-famed oracle of Delphi, and asked that his son might speak aloud. The seeress, gazing with prophetic eye into the future, returned this answer:—

> " Wide ruling Lydian, in thy wishes wild,
>   Ask not to hear the accents of thy child ;
>   Far better is his silence for thy peace,
>   And sad will be the day when that shall cease."

Years passed, and fortune frowned on the great king. His enemies besieged and captured his capital. A common soldier meeting him in the street, and not knowing who it was, drew his sword to kill him. Suddenly the dumb son, who was with him, called out in a loud voice, " Oh man, do not kill Crœsus," and saved his father's life. Ever afterwards his speech was restored.

Modern experience teaches us that these strange, almost miraculous cures can be brought about by a simple and ready means—electricity. Pass the electric current along the vocal chords within the throat, and the patient, who has not spoken above her breath for months or years, will often address you at once in her natural voice. At other times, loss of voice is associated with serious disorder of the throat and lungs, and is next to hopeless.

Lisping is a confusion of the sounds s and th. Taken early in life, it is readily amended. If a child is thoroughly drilled in the pronunciation of Greek, he will surely break the habit.

Certain odors and articles of food should be shunned by those who wish to preserve their voice in full health The fumes of an extinguished candle, any rank smoke, gas, or vapor, are very injurious. Even the most fragrant Havana must be condemned from this point of view. Tobacco smoke should be shunned by a singer. Acid fruits, and such as contain pungent oils, are also injurious. Walnuts, almonds, and pecan-nuts have an especially bad reputation here, whether justly or not we cannot say.

OFFENSIVE BREATH.

A "bad breath," as it is popularly called, is such a serious misfortune that we devote a separate section to its consideration. Many an one who would be an engaging companion is rendered intolerable by it, by it many a damsel estranges her lover, many a wife her husband.

We have termed it a misfortune. This is not quite correct. It is often a fault, one that could and should be remedied. Knowing how common it is, how nauseous it is to associates, how mortifying to the individual herself, we have given close attention to its various causes in order to suggest remedies wherever remedies are of any avail. Often the first whiff of a fetid breath will reveal its origin, and if blindfolded one can prescribe the proper means by which it can be alleviated.

The great majority of cases arise either from the lungs, the stomach, or the teeth. When from the lungs, the odor is of a sickening sweetish character; when from the stomach, it is marked by the presence of that gas known as sulphuretted hydrogen, which we are most familiar with from its presence in rotten eggs; when from the teeth, it is putrescent, reminding one of decaying animal tissue. It may also be produced from diseases within the nostrils, or the throat, or from several of these causes combined.

Unfortunate, indeed, is the young lady who is thus made an object of disgust to her social companions. It is her duty to herself and to society to use every self-denial, every resource in her power to remedy this defect. The most polite of men cannot overcome their aversion so long as it continues.

It is related of Benserade, court poet of Louis XIV., that he was obliged on one occasion to stand close to a lady whose breath was unpleasant, while she was singing a piece of her own composition. When she had finished, a bystander asked the poet what he thought of the piece and the artist.

"Mademoiselle," he replied, "has an excellent voice, her words are well-chosen, but her air is frightful."

The pun was not lost on those who happened to be in front of the singer.

Worse consequences may ensue than to become the target of unfeeling jests. We know the instance of a physician who lost one after another of his cases of confinement, until the number was over forty. They all succumbed to puerperal fever. He took every conceivable precaution; bathed, shaved even his hair, left the city for a week, all in vain. The reason was he had that disease "ozæna," which we have previously described, and into whatever room he entered, he carried a breath that poisoned its atmosphere.

If it is the teeth that are at fault, they should be put under the care of an approved dentist to extract, fill, or treat in what manner their condition demands. When the cause is in the stomach, usually some form of dyspepsia is present; water and gases rise to the mouth, the body is constipated, and a general sense of unpleasantness is felt in body and mind. This condition requires the enlightened care of the physician, whose duty it becomes to define to himself the precise character of the dyspepsia, to seek its origin, and to address to its cure those remedies which a mature experience has placed at his command. There are, we may add for the benefit of sufferers, comparatively few instances where, with a hearty and intelligent co-operation on their part, any failure will take place in treating these cases.

We cannot speak such cheering words to those who owe their offensive breath to the condition of the lungs. With them a grave malady is threatening, or is actually in progress. Their battle is no longer for good looks; it is for dear life. By timely and judicious provisions they may forestall the foe who is insidiously stealing upon them. They may escape him by a flight to the sunny shores of Florida, or the dry plains of the northwest. But their welfare is too imminently endangered to permit them to trifle or to experiment.[1]

---

[1] See on the subject of the treatment of consumption in its early stages, and the advantages of a change of climate, DR.

Those who owe their breath to chronic catarrh, to
ozæna, or to some growth within the nose, may make
up their minds to perhaps a protracted, but an ultimately successful treatment, and should lose no time
in commencing it.

These are general directions, looking toward a radical cure. Now we shall give some suitable to those
cases where an unpleasant breath is not permanent,
and not indicative of any serious disturbance of the
system. For instance, in some ladies it only appears
after a late supper, after eating some peculiar article
of food, or at certain periodical times.

If it is supposed to be connected with the teeth, or
the secretions of the mouth, the following mouth-wash
will be found most efficacious :—

| Permanganate of potash | one grain ; |
| Rose-water | one ounce. |

Rinse the mouth well every few hours.

The objection to this excellent mixture is, that it
stains slightly the teeth, but the discoloration may
readily be removed by a tooth-sponge or brush ; but so
far from injuring, it will be of great service in preserving them, and in preventing or relieving toothache.
If the taste is unpleasant, a few drops of oil of peppermint or teaberry will conceal it. It is much better

D. G. BRINTON, "Guide-Book of Florida and the South,"
Phila., 1869.

13

than the washes often recommended, containing chlorinated lime, which attacks the enamel. The following wash may also be used safely:—

Chlorate of potash   two drachms;
Rose-water   six ounces.

Distilled water of any other flavor may be substituted.

Various substances are in vogue to sweeten the breath, and to conceal either its naturally unpleasant odor, or some acquired scent, as of onions, tobacco, spirits, etc. The most elegant are cachous, troches, and lozenges, made chiefly of catechu, charcoal, gum tragacanth, or liquorice, flavored with aromatic essential oils. Cardamom seed, cloves, and allspice, are altogether too vulgar, too commonly seen on fashionable drinking bars, for any lady to have recourse to them. One might, horrible to suggest, suspect her of having been indulging in a little gin-and-water, or some such tipple. Coffee grains, fresh-roasted, have a high reputation for masking completely the scent, either of spirits or of onions. and having little odor of their own. Our observation leads us to believe that this is not undeserved. What we place equal reliance in, is the Canada snakeroot (*Asarum Canadense*, U. S. P.), a small portion of which can be chewed, or the root powdered and made into a lozenge. It leaves a fresh, cool, pleasant taste, and imparts a faintly spicy aroma to the breath.

If there is a foul stomach, with a taste and odor of

stale eggs, a wineglassful of water containing three grains of chloride of lime (*Calx chlorinata,* U. S. P.) should be swallowed several times a day, and the diet limited to easily digestible food, of which charcoal, either in the form of "charcoal crackers," or burnt toast, should figure conspicuously. Any irregularities of food, drink, or sleep must be corrected, the natural functions regulated, and the skin kept in activity by frequent baths, and rubbing with a flesh-glove or coarse towel. A draught containing twenty grains of the bisulphite of soda has also an excellent effect on offensive breath arising from this cause. It may be taken, masked with essence of peppermint, twice daily.

THE ARM AND HAND.

THE ARM.

THE "upper extremity," as anatomists call it, by
which they mean the arm, forearm, and hand, is
so constantly brought into prominence in daily life that
its care and embellishment become almost a weighty
matter. If we divide the distance from the top of the
shoulder to the end of the middle finger into fourteen
equal parts, the length of the hand ought to equal
three parts, the forearm five parts, and the arm above
the elbow six parts.

While moderate exercise improves the arm by en-
larging symmetrically all the muscles, it is not in good
taste for a woman to display a brawny, sinewy member. It must have a roundness, one gentle curve
sinking into another, which is not consistent with great
muscular development. Constant and regular use
will most surely tend to give a correct shape.

Bracelets should not be worn tight enough to affect

(148)

the circulation, nor loose enough to rub on the wrist
joint. If, as is sometimes the case, they cause an
irritation of the skin, they should be laid aside altogether.

Many a fine lady takes more pride in a beautiful
hand than in any other feature of her person. "Good
Queen Bess," royal old coquette that she was, is an
example in point. At her levees she used to take care
to have one of her hands prominently displayed. They
were small, white, soft, and well proportioned, so she
had a right to be proud of them.

To have such a delicate hand as hers is not in the
power of every one. Most of us are under the law of
toil, and bear upon us the indelible imprint of our
handicrafts. An eminent French surgeon has asserted
that by the inspection of this member alone he can
tell, nine times out of ten, what is the avocation of the
individual. Every trade, every employment—except
the tread-mill—calls for some assistance from the hand
—that "divine tool," as old Aristotle called it. "The
miller's thumb," broad and flattened with testing of
the grain between it and the forefinger, is a proverbial
expression. The fiddler's left hand, with its flattened
and horny finger tips, betrays his trade. Shakspeare,
in that touching sonnet which reveals the bitterness
with which he saw himself, with all his divine spirit,

13*

forced to dress as a clown, and tickle a dull crowd to laughter for a sustenance, exclaims:—

> " Thence comes it that my name receives a brand,
> And almost thence my nature is subdued
> To what it works in, like the dyer's hand."

Lifting heavy objects, sweeping, washing, scrubbing, when long continued, and especially during growth, destroy the admired shape and elegant contour. The hand of little use not only has the daintier touch but the daintier form; the fingers are round and tapering, the joints are small, the skin smooth, the lines shallow. In the words of Ariosto, it is:—

> " Lunghetta alquanto e di larghezza angusta."

Compare such a one with the hand of a washer-woman, and note how beauty wins through idleness. Does the game pay for the candle? Ah! that is a serious question, which each must decide for herself.

Even the lighter employments deform, to some extent, this complex member. In writing, if the pen is held awkwardly, or in a cramped position, it will soon leave a slight disfigurement. A too small thimble will distort the finger tips. Rings are often left on the fingers until they are half buried in a deep crease, and it is next to impossible to remove them. The arm should be elevated and the finger soaked in ice-water for ten or fifteen minutes, then immediately anointed with glycerine, and the ring slipped off. If this fails, the finger should be very tightly wrapped in fine, strong, well-waxed sewing silk from the tip upward; when the ring is reached, the end of the silk should be slipped beneath it with a blunt bodkin, and then, as the string is unwound, the ring will be forced down. Sometimes even this does not succeed, and the ring has to be filed off, or what is far better, thoroughly cleansed with ether, and rubbed with quicksilver for some minutes, when it will readily fall to pieces, and can be thus removed without pain, delay, or exertion.

We have known at least one instance where the hand had become puffy and ill-shaped by wearing gloves fastened too tightly across the wrist. And we remember seeing President Lincoln's right hand on one occasion when it was actually swollen by a series of violent hand-shaking. Why is it that this absurd custom of "paddling palms" has been allowed to become so universal among us? It is a severe infliction on public men. General George Washington, it is well known, had a strong aversion to it, and at his levees always stood with his hands behind him, simply bowing with dignified courtesy as one after another was presented. Our best society, we are glad to see, are discountenancing hand-shaking as a general custom, and reserve it for a mark of personal, kindly feeling.

It is needless to emphasize the importance of the use of gloves. The best are those of animal fibre, as kid, doeskin, or buckskin. The court ladies in old times probably could never boast of their pretty white hands, for the fashion of wearing gloves in full dress was first introduced in England by Anne Boleyn, the unfortunate queen of Henry the Eighth. They were not at all popular at first, and the great ladies of the court, jealous that the country girl become a queen should thus outstrip them in the arts of beauty, circulated the report that she had six fingers, and took this mode of concealing the deformity.

In later days the fops transcended the belles in their mania for this luxury. Beau Brummell and the Count d'Orsay each used to wear six different pairs daily, and never put on the same pair twice.

Softness and whiteness of the hands are prized by every beauty, and many a one who don't pretend to be a beauty. It is supposed to be something difficult to attain. Not at all. In the first place, do not expose them to the wind and sun too freely. Never employ strong soaps, or hard water.

"But if the water *is* hard?"

Put a teaspoonful of powdered borax in the basin.

"And if we have no borax? A lady don't carry a drug-store with her on her travels."

Don't wash the hands. It is as a rule superfluous, in fact an injury, from a cosmetic point of view, this constant moistening the skin.

The Baron Alibert was some years since the most celebrated of all the Parisian surgeons for treating diseases of the skin. One day a lady said to him:—

"Doctor, how white and smooth your hands are. Why don't you tell us your secret for keeping them so?"

"Madam," replied the doctor, "if I were to tell you, you would not believe me; or at any rate you would not imitate me."

"Oh yes I will, doctor; *do* tell me."

"I *never* wash them ——"

"What!"

"With water."

"With what then?"

"With the best olive oil of Aix. Don't you remember that the ancient athletes anointed themselves daily with oil? You may be sure those gallants were never troubled with skin diseases."

Since Baron Alibert's time we have discovered something even better than the oil of Aix; it is glycerine. A bottle of pure glycerine—but *chemically pure*, remember, without any of those salts of lime or of lead which are found in much of the glycerine sold, and which will discolor and irritate the skin—should form an indispensable adjunct in every lady's toilet set. A tablespoonful of it in a pint of water will soften and protect the hand from the air. It should be rubbed in, but not wiped off.

To whiten the hands promptly, five or six grains of chlorinated lime may be dissolved in the water, which in all cases should be as near the temperature of the body as may be. The lotions which contain corrosive sublimate, sometimes recommended, must be heedfully used, as we have known them, even when very weak, to irritate the skin violently.

Not at all dangerous, and of good service in rendering the hands soft and smooth, is this perhaps familiar recipe: Take horse-chestnuts, peel and dry them thoroughly in the oven. Pound or grind them into a fine powder. Put a tablespoonful into the wash-water, whenever the hands are rinsed.

Here is another wash which has been deservedly praised, not only for preventing redness of the hands, but for improving the skin, and destroying warts :—

Muriate of ammonia	a teaspoonful ;
Aromatic vinegar	a tablespoonful ;
Tepid soft water	a quart.

Soak the hands in this for ten or fifteen minutes morning and evening.

The use of " cosmetic gloves," as they are called, has long been known in some countries, and there are ladies who glove themselves as regularly on retiring to bed, as they do on going into the street. These gloves, when designed simply to soften and whiten the hands, are prepared by brushing the inside of a pair of stout kid or dog-skin gloves with the following mixture :—

Yelk of two fresh eggs,	
Oil of sweet almonds, of each two tablespoonfuls ;	
Tincture of benzoin	a dessertspoonful ;
Rose-water	a tablespoonful.

Beat them well together, and keep in a closely corked bottle. The gloves should be freshly painted every night, and the same pair should not be used longer than two weeks.

When some disease of the skin is present, the gloves can be brushed with some more active preparation than that mentioned above.

Gloves made of India-rubber are largely used in perference to those of skin for wearing at night. They confine the perspiration, and thus keep the skin bathed in moist warmth, rendering it softer, whiter, and more delicate. They are also of considerable efficacy in some cutaneous eruption, and for chapped hands.

A clammy moisture of the hands is an annoyance with which some are afflicted. Possibly it is a sign of enfeebled health, but it may occur as a constitutional tendency. The lotion which we have just mentioned, containing muriate of ammonia, does efficient service here, too. So will half a teaspoonful of alum in the water, or rendering it sour with a few drops of aromatic sulphuric acid. For temporary purposes, the hands may be rubbed with French chalk (powdered soap-stone), or the "lycopodium" powder, which is the product of a curious Alpine moss.

For "chapped" hands, pure glycerine, well rubbed in several times a day, cannot be improved upon, though sometimes it is necessary to follow up this with wearing gloves of caoutchouc cloth at night. The late celebrated actress, Madame Vestris, was said to wrap her hands every night in thin slices of fresh meat. This was not nice, nor a particle more efficient than to anoint them with fresh olive oil or pure glycerine, and then, without wiping, draw on the caoutchouc gloves. Fresh, unsalted butter is likewise an admirable ointment, but lard or cold cream, which is often made from coarse, half rancid, but highly scented animal fats, should be shunned.

The hands are subject to a great number of deformities. A French surgeon has recently written a book of nigh three hundred pages on them. That is as much as saying we do not intend to dilate upon them here. In remedying them, it is not enough that the surgeon should seek to re-establish the use of the member. He should also seek to restore its beauty. This is too generally lost sight of. Here, as elsewhere, the claims of cosmetic surgery are apt to be disregarded, to the subsequent annoyance of the patient.

One of the commonest deformities is enlarged joints. Chronic rheumatism and hard work are their parents. There is not much to be done for them.

For warts, however, which are infinitely more common, household remedies are as plenty as blackberries. We tried the following in our young days. prescribed by an old family servant: Steal a piece of fresh meat. Cut it into as many fragments as you have warts. Bury the fragments under a stone. As fast as they decay, your warts will disappear. Owing to our bad success, and to a due respect for the statutes of this commonwealth concerning misprision of felony, we have not recommended it in our practice. We prefer to touch them repeatedly with chromic acid, or tinctture of iodine (the colorless tincture, which leaves no unsightly stain, and which it is always best to employ on external parts), or with nitrate of silver. With one or other of these means they are sure to take their departure before long, and, curiously enough, as if they were in some occult sympathy, when one goes they usually all go. Another very efficient means is to treat them to a current of electricity daily. When in very great numbers internal remedies must be employed, for which the family physician should be consulted.

THE NAILS.

The nails should be oval in form, pink in color, with a white crescent at their base, and evenly cut a little below the tip of the finger. They should be frequently cleansed with the nail brush, which should be soft, and not stiff and harsh, as most of them are. The thin skin should be pressed away from their roots so as to display the pearly half moon there situated, and, by thus lengthening the oval of the nail, to give the finger a more tapering appearance. Often, too, this little

14

attention prevents those very painful affections known as " hang nails" or " ag nails."

The most elegant hint we can offer concerning the color of the nails is to polish them now and then—not too often. It may be done by rubbing them length-wise with a soft sponge dipped in emery dust tinged with vermilion or carmine. This lends them a delicate, roseate hue. No one must ever think of scraping them with a knife or a bit of glass, as this may lead to troublesome diseases.

An equally excellent nail powder, and the one commonly sold in the shops, is oxide of tin, perfumed and colored with carmine. A little of it can be rubbed on the nail with a finger of the other hand, or with a piece of chamois leather. It soon renders the surface smooth, bright, and pink, which is not surprising, since this is the substance used to polish tortoise shell and horns.

The school-girl habit of biting the nails must be broken up at once. If in children, rub a little extract of quassia on the finger tips. This is so bitter that they are careful not to taste it twice. Not only the nails, but the beauty of the whole finger and hand, is often forfeited by neglect in this respect.

Sometimes the nails become brittle, crack, and break off readily in irregular pieces. This is a trouble diffi-cult to manage, and demands long medical treatment.

Consumption is often accompanied with a deformity

of the nails. They grow curved over the ends of the fingers and are usually in perceptible ridges.

Of course more serious matters than the treatment of the local malformation demand our attention when this is the case.

THE LEG AND FOOT

THE LEG.

THE author of that excellent little book "Vulgarisms and other Errors of Speech," censures with just severity the American prudery which substitutes in conversation, "limb," or "extremity," for leg. The latter is the proper and the only proper word, and those who shun it so anxiously lead one to suspect that they are in the habit of indulging unbecoming thoughts. Like that literary prude, who once said to Dr. Johnson, the lexicographer:—

"Doctor, I am *so* much pleased with your Dictionary, and especially because you have omitted all improper words."

"So, madam," replied the caustic old humorist, "you searched for them, did you?"

In anatomy, the leg extends from the knee downward, the thigh from the knee upward, and both these, together with the foot, are called "the lower extremity," or "the lower limb." The bones of this extremity are differently arranged in woman and in man. One of the consequences of this is that no woman can run gracefully. They run, says a witty Frenchman, as if they intended to be overtaken.

The knee should be midway between the lower line of the body and the ground. Below the knee the calf should rise rapidly, full and round, and taper gently to a slender ankle.

A handsome leg is a rarity, we had almost said an impossibility, among American women. The reason of this is the place where they wear their garters. No Frenchwoman, no Englishwoman of cultivation, now-a-days wears her garter below the knee. It is ruinous to the shape of the calf. More than this, it has serious consequences of another kind. The principal vein of the leg (*vena saphena brevis*) runs just beneath the skin until it nearly reaches the knee, when it sinks between the muscles. Now if this is constricted at its largest part by a tight garter, the blood is checked in its return to the heart, the feet are easily chilled, and more liable to disease, the other veins of the leg are swollen into hard, blue knots, become varicose, as it is called, and often break, forming obstinate ulcers. This is a picture which a physician sees nearly every day.

With the garter fastened above the knee all this pain and deformity is avoided.

An ungraceful carriage is sometimes owing to "bow-legs," or "bandy-legs." This condition is brought about by allowing children to walk too soon. Every mother should be on her guard against it, as it is a source of much mortification, and cannot completely be hidden even by long dresses. Nothing can remedy it.

False calves, manufactured of cork, and fastened to the leg beneath the stocking, are a device of the toilet which we have never, to our knowledge, observed out of Paris, and which might as well be allowed to remain as one of the peculiar features of that great capital.

THE FOOT AND SHOE.

A pretty foot, says Goethe, is the one element of beauty which defies the assaults of age. If properly cared for, it remains as perfect at seventy as it was at seventeen. We have the cheering certainty, therefore, that the attention we bestow on it will repay us as long as we live.

Yet how little do we give to it! What a sight it is in bathing hours on the sea-beach, to see the distorted, red, corned, bunioned, and swollen feet of the bathers! No wonder "corn-doctors" do a thriving business, and can build handsome houses on their neighbors' toes!

A well-formed foot is scarcely to be found in modern civilization. The late actress, Madame Vestris, whom we have already mentioned, was said to have had the handsomest of any woman of her day—so far as the observers could learn. She devoted uncommon care to its preservation. She always wore white satin slippers, exquisitely fitted, and not laced or buttoned, but *sewed* on every morning, and ripped off at night. So she wore a new pair every day.

The foot should be slender, rounded, in length a little less than one-eighth of the height of the body, the heel only slightly prominent, and the middle of the foot arched.

A flat foot has never been admired. It is brought about either by carrying heavy burdens, or wearing ill-shaped shoes. Therefore the arched foot used to be considered a sign of high-birth, and delicate breeding. In Spain, one of the proofs of ancient lineage, of true old "*sangre azul,*" was to stand on a marble pavement, and let a tiny stream of water flow under the arch of the foot without wetting it.

If the natural beauty of this member is so much defaced, the shoemakers must answer for it. Their art is wofully behind the age in an æsthetic as well as a hygienic point of view. We cannot reform them, and we don't intend to try, so we shall content ourselves with giving a few hints to those who would display their feet to the best advantage, and preserve them in the most comfort.

First, then, every one with the slightest wish for either of these good things, should have a *last* made for his own use. We can never find a perfectly fitting shoe in a ready made shoe store. That is readily granted. Neither can we have one made on an old last. The feet of no two persons are exactly alike, so no last can fit them both.

Thus, too, a foot always shows its own delicate natural form.

Not that we urge any departure from the prevailing style of shoe. If carefully fitted, they will answer very well, although some female reformers have declared their independence of them. A distinguished woman who not long since returned from Europe, told a friend of ours, of an interview with Miss Florence Nightingale. During the conversation she could not help but notice the singular shape of that eminent lady's foot. She had never heard that Miss Nightingale was lame, or mal-formed, but certainly something was the matter. Her curiosity prompted her to inquire of some mutual friend, who at once explained that Miss Nightingale, despising the modern instrument of torture vended by fashionable shoemakers, is accustomed to plant her stocking foot firmly on a piece of leather, draw the outline of the figure it forms, and have her shoe made to correspond exactly with it!

The heel should neither be very high nor narrow, as this throws the body forward, impairs the gracefulness of the carriage, and is also apt to predispose the ankle to " turn" or give way, which is both awkward

and painful. The centre of the sole should rise above
both heel and toe on the inside of the shoe, so as to
preserve the arch of the foot.

Our next subject is a tender one—not love, as you
will at once guess, but—corns. They are the Nemesis
which visits infraction of the rules we have just laid
down. So common are they that in all our large cities
there are individuals who devote themselves to their
extraction, and make a living by it. These gentlemen
are not always too implicitly to be relied upon. Some,
indeed, are skilful and reputable specialists, but the
majority are ignorant and tricky, thinking of nothing
but how to "make business," that immortal principle
which Charles Dickens says is the only stable and
entirely certain one in English law. We had recently
in our hands a small book published by one of them in
which he urgently dissuades any one from cutting their
own corns, but always to come to the celebrated chiro-
podist, Dr. ———, to have it done ($5.00, if you
please).

This is charlatanism. Every person can not only
cut, but cure their corns, if they will take the
trouble. They can even learn to extract them on the
feet of others, but not readily on their own. The
method is simple, the operation painless, and we shall
describe it.

The only instruments needed are a pair of small steel
forceps, and two or three blunt-pointed steel or silver

instruments, technically called quadrilles. The corn is first softened by immersion in warm water, or by a drop of oil or glycerine. The foot is then held in a good light, and the centre of the corn loosened by passing the point of the quadrille gently around the circumference of the callous portion. This is seized by the forceps, and held to one side while the instruments loosen the other side. So the operation is continued, very gently and leisurely, until the whole callus is loosened and the corn picked out by the forceps. Under ordinary circumstances not the least pain need be given and not a drop of blood shed. This is the art and the mystery of corn doctoring.

It requires some skill, some command over the fingers and the nerves; it cannot be performed on one's self. This is disappointing. But we have not yet divulged all the "tricks of the trade." Here are some methods of curing one's own proper and peculiar corns without assistance from any one.

Take several small pieces of ordinary sticking plaster. Cut in them holes the size of the corn. Apply one over the other so as to surround the corn, but leave it exposed. Then in the opening drop a saturated solution of caustic soda, and cover with a thin piece of plaster. Renew this every other day for eight or ten days, and the corn will be gone.

Or cut the corn carefully with a knife not too sharp, taking care that it is not cut to the quick or to blood.

Then touch it lightly with nitrate of silver in stick. In two or three days a dark, callous crust will cover the surface. Remove this with the knife, and apply a second time the silver nitrate. Do this for a fortnight, and if it is judiciously and regularly done, and the part protected from pressure, it will cure any corn.

Very painful corns can be helped by being covered with the following plaster, though we have little faith in its curative powers:—

Resin plaster	one ounce ;
Melt and stir in	
Muriate of ammonia	two drachms ;
Powdered opium	one drachm.

The strong tincture of iodine applied daily is often an efficient remedy, and another is to rub them morning and night with a piece of pumice-stone. If well softened beforehand, this latter method, though tedious, is satisfactory and painless. It is particularly suited to soft corns between the toes.

A word concerning the cutting of corns. There is a right and a wrong way to do even this. Bear in mind that the part of the growth which is thick and painful is not near the edges, but in the centre. Therefore, they should be pared into a concave or funnel shape; not flat across, but deeper in the middle than at the circumference.

A bunion is a corn on a large scale, which has its seat on the outer side of the joint of the great toe.

As soon as there are any signs of their advent, a small, flat, hollow ring of India rubber should be worn to prevent pressure from the shoe. When once formed they can be reduced by assiduous poulticing, and touching with nitrate of silver, tincture of iodine, or chromic acid. Sometimes they become violently inflamed, and then it is best to call in a surgeon, for grave injury of the joint may result, if they are neglected or ill-treated.

A sleigh ride or a skating party leaves many a delightful reminiscence, and sometimes one that is not delightful, to wit, *chilblains.* They are the result of frosted feet, and keep up a burning and stinging for months, whenever the foot becomes warm. There are numerous domestic remedies in vogue for their prevention and cure. Soaking the feet in water in which potatoes have been boiled, in strong brine, in bran-water containing several teaspoonfuls of muriate of ammonia, rubbing them with oil of turpentine, all have their advocates among those respectable old ladies who are rich in domestic lore, and all occasionally do wonders. A more unfailing remedy will be found in keeping the parts moist with this lotion :—

White Castile soap	a drachm ;
Milder solution of ammonia	two drachms ;
Tincture of cantharides	two ounces.

Or if it is too inconvenient to keep up an application of this nature, the frost-bitten parts may be painted morning and evening with equal parts of tincture of iodine and solution of ammonia, which, after all, is perhaps the best means we have yet suggested.

We spoke at considerable length about offensive breath, but the odor of *fetid feet* is still less tolerable. It is impossible, with any comfort, to sleep in the same room with a person so afflicted, and not a few married women have traced their domestic unhappiness to this cause. It is not owing to lack of cleanliness, though this accusation is ever laid at the door of the unfortunate sufferers. The disturbed secretions of the skin may be at fault, and these must be changed ere we can look for any permanent amendment. This is a question for the physician, as the fetor is often connected with disease elsewhere, which must first be remedied.

But we can offer some excellent suggestions as palliatives. The stockings must be woollen, and changed daily, and the shoes frequently. The latter should be large enough to admit a thin sole of felt, which should be steeped several times a week in a solution of permanganate of potash, twenty grains to the ounce, and then dried and inserted. Several pairs of such soles should be kept on hand. The feet themselves should be washed morning and evening in cold water, containing a few teaspoonfuls of alum, then well dried and anointed thoroughly with the following ointment:—

Ointment of oxide of zinc	one ounce;
Crystallized carbolic acid	five grains.

15

In one instance of a young lady, faultless in the cares of the toilette, seemingly in excellent health, but with such an offensive perspiration to her feet that she could not remain at boarding-school, we tried with complete success, so far as we have since learned, the troublesome but efficient method recommended by the distinguished Professor Hebra, of Vienna. It is by means of strapping the foot assiduously with diachylon plaster, after having smeared it thoroughly with an alterative mercurial ointment.

The care of the toe-nails is essentially the same as that of the finger-nails, and should occupy quite as prominent a place in the daily duties of the toilette. They should be kept clean, cut a little shorter than the toe itself, the skin prevented from encroaching upon them, and occasionally polished with a little nail powder.

Sometimes the nail, especially that of the great toe, grows into the flesh, causing a most painful sore. The surgeon's remedy is to tear out the whole nail, or one half of it, with the tweezers. Patients, however, are not easily persuaded to submit to this, and we recommend, therefore, the method of bandaging. This is done by placing a small pad firmly against the flesh, and binding it in that position by adhesive plaster. We have also used, both alone and in connection with bandages, the sesquichloride of iron, which destroys the vitality and sensitiveness of the flesh without causing any pain.

Of the many deformities to which the foot is subject, such as club-foot, enlarged joints, tumors, and so forth, we shall say nothing. They belong, indeed, within the scope of cosmetic surgery, but to that higher branch of it which demands earnest study and professional skill, not to that which any intelligent individual may compass. Suffice it to say that modern art has devised many means by which such malformations may be redressed, and the crooked made straight, promptly and without causing pain. Therefore, those who are thus afflicted should not be deterred from taking proper advice, and obtaining that large increase in the beauty and usefulness of the member which they may legitimately expect. Orthopedic surgeons of repute can be found in all our large cities.

THE SKIN AND COMPLEXION.

A CHARMING subject, this of beauty, you would think, and one that ought to inspire the prosiest pen; but in fact, when Destiny decreed that we should read up the literature that concerns it, she condemned us to the perusal of many a dry page. We say this in order to speak of one of the exceptions. This is the little book of Jacob le Bibliophile, *Confessions archéologiques et cosmetiques.* It is both witty and learned.

Everybody who knows that old bookworm, knows that he is an original thinker. He has his own views about beauty too.

"Beauty," he tells you, "is simply—the skin. Resolve me the problem of preserving the skin, and the preservation of beauty is no longer a problem."

"Thus it is easy to foresee the time when all women will be beautiful, for, without a doubt, certain precautions carefully conned and punctually observed, will maintain the lustre and fresh hue of youth and health.

(172)

"I tell you we shall certainly have the Age of Beauty, and it will come, I fear me, before the Age of Wit, or the Age of Virtue, or the Age of Happiness."

This prophecy of the venerable *lifre-lofre* so cheers us, that we continue our labors with a feeling as if we were the heralds sent to announce the great time coming, when there shall be no more rivalry among the belles, for they shall all be equally lovely. Mindful of his definition of beauty, we shall be very minute in what we have to say about the skin.

What is the skin?

Any doctor will answer you with alacrity, that it is the protecting cover to the exterior of the body, that it is composed of two layers, the epidermis or scarf-skin on the outside, a structure usually thin and without sensation, and the derma or true skin, a sensitive layer of fibres with minute eminences, immediately beneath the epidermis. The epidermis is composed of numerous cells. These contain the coloring matter which gives the dark hue to the brunette, and to the brown and black races of men. It is the epidermis which rises when a blister has "drawn." Blister a negro, and when the epidermis comes away, you will find the spot is white. His color, which we make such an ado about, is not even skin-deep; it is barely scarf-skin-deep.

So it is with freckles, moles, moths, and most kind of spots on the skin. They are very superficial, and do not affect the true skin at all. Here is matter for wholesale consolation. For where is the lady who has not on some part one or a dozen of these blemishes she fain would get rid of? In point of looks, it is the scarf-skin much more than the true skin which concerns us, for it is this outer and ever visible layer which is most frequently to blame in unhandsome complexions.

With a becoming sense, therefore, of the weighty matters we are about to handle, we shall pass in review all the means which are useful in retaining and defending against the envious assaults of Time, the clear and brilliant complexion of youth, that

"Beauty truly blent, whose red and white
Nature's own sweet and cunning hand lays on."

Nor will our task end here. He is unworthy the name of physician, who concerns himself only about those who are whole. We shall go further, and turning to those whom the old fellow with hour-glass and sickle has already worsted, we shall ransack for their sakes the magazine of art for means to repair, or if repairing is out of the question, then to conceal, the damage they have sustained in the conflict of years. For if it is well for age to take lessons from the buoyant spirits and active mind of youth, may it not with equal propriety strive for the bright eye and healthful glow? The imitation is not what repels us; it is the failure in the attempt at imitation.

Our instructions commence with a homely theme, but an orthodox one. It is cleanliness of the person; in short

WASHING AND BATHING.

Baron Liebig says that the progress of nations in civilization can be accurately measured by the amount of soap they use. If the test were applied, we fear our country would make a poor figure. In this city of seven hundred thousand bodies there is not a single public bath. Even in " good society" (save the mark) there is not that attention to scrupulous cleanliness which there should be. More than one young lady might find a moral in the anecdote told of Lady Mary Wortley Montague. When young, this famous woman seems to have been a model of candor, if not of neatness. One day a companion ventured to suggest to her that her hands needed washing.

" My hands!" exclaimed she, " what would you say if you saw my feet?"

We rarely prophesy. But we confidently pronounce one prediction which is worth all those contained in the folios of that renowned cosmetic artist, who afterwards turned astrologist and prophet, Michael Nostradamus. It is this:—

The age of beauty will never come until every woman takes a bath every day, when she is in health.

The bath, moreover, must be in water slightly tepid,

but *not* warm, and of waters, one kind is superior to all others.

Here, at last, is the secret of Diana of Poictiers.

Every morning of her life, that lady bathed in *rain-water;* "and this it was, I swear by the soul of my honored mistress," says master Oudard, her apothe-cary-in-chief, surgeon-barber, and perfumer, as he delights to call himself, "that was the only secret which that illustrious dame employed to preserve her health, youth, and beauty to the age of threescore and twelve years."

We believe the honest apothecary, for this is distilled water, perfectly neutral and pure, fitted beyond any other to render the skin clean, odorless, white, soft, smooth, and transparent. Let it be preferred to all others, for it is better than any of them. When it cannot be obtained, soft water will answer, but hard water, which contains mineral salts, should be avoided, as it cracks and injures the epidermis. Is not such a secret worth more than gold, whether soluble or insoluble? For beauty is not a thing of price.

A cold bath does not suit many constitutions, and is not advisable for the skin. Still more objectionable is one which is hot. The water should be tepid, and in using it, one should wet the person sufficiently to loosen the scales of the scarf-skin, and then rub the flesh, not violently, but gently and for some time, with a coarse towel, a soft flesh-brush, or a flesh-mitten not too rough. A healthy glow should be felt after the rubbing, and the skin should be pink and warm. If it seems dry and harsh afterwards, an ounce or two of glycerine can be put in the water, or a small quantity rubbed in with the hand. If, on the contrary, there remains a greasy feeling and a shiny appearance on the surface, a few teaspoonfuls of spirit of ammonia may be poured in the water, or some common yellow soap employed daily. It has also been recommended that persons with skins of this description should, after drying themselves thoroughly, dust the surface with a bag containing finely powdered starch and orris-root, three parts of the former to one of the latter.

History says that when Anne Boleyn came to France then a young girl, lady of honor to Mary, Queen of Louis XII., she was of a "dark and oily" complexion. Some one recommended a daily bath, and after the bath a powder such as we have described. When a year or two afterwards she returned to England, there was not a lady at the Court of Henry VIII, who compared with her in beauty of complexion, and that king, who was a connoisseur in such matters, soon showed that he indorsed the general sentiment. It was an unlucky success for her, as all the world knows; but she never blamed her beauty for her misfortunes. Quite the contrary, for the story goes that on the day before her death she said to her tire-women:—

"It is high time that the headsman did his work, for

I have not a grain of powder left, and the king would doubtless carry his cruelty to the extent of not allowing me any more."

The bath had probably more to do with it than the powder, for think a moment what a bath does. Do you know why of all parts of the body the face is most subject to spots, pimples, and similar eruptions? You probably think it is simply the aggravating way of matters in general. No such thing. It is because the face is washed oftener, the pores are kept open, and the circulation stimulated by the rubbing, so that the effete humors in the blood find there a readier exit, and consequently crowd thither from all parts of the body, giving the skin there too much to do. Wash and rub daily all parts of the surface, and the secretions will be equally distributed, and no one part overtasked.

Many things have been suggested besides water for bathing purposes. There was Prince Jerome Bonaparte, who took a bath daily, the spendthrift, in wine, and that wine champagne. Even during the fearful Russian campaign he did not intermit, or but a very short time, this unheard-of luxury. Whether it had anything to do with preserving him to the age of seventy-six, we do not know.

The juices of certain fruits, especially raspberries and strawberries, have been lauded as sovereign washes for the skin, but this is a vagary of fashion of no practical moment.

Baths of milk merit more serious attention. They date back into ancient times, and many a high-born dame of Rome and Athens practised her ablutions in this nourishing fluid. It was supposed to give the skin a peculiar softness and freshness, unequalled by any other application. This may be true, for Madame de Genlis relates in her Memoirs that on one occasion the fancy took her to try this experiment. She sent to the neighboring farm-houses, bought up some twenty or thirty gallons, and took a royal bath. She describes her sensations for hours after as most pleasant and exhilarating.

Another lady of her day, the Princess Borghese, afterwards Queen of Naples, was said to indulge regularly in a milk-bath. So essential did she deem it to her comfort, or else to her good looks, that she denied herself a visit to the Court of St. James, simply because she heard that in England she must forego her luxurious habit.

The custom is not yet extinct in Paris. We were told when there that a number of fashionable ladies continue it. Knowing that milk sold at fifteen sous a litre, or thereabout, we remarked that it must be an expensive indulgence.

"Not very," replied our informant, with the utmost coolness, "the milk is afterwards bought up by the second class *laiteries*, and served out to their customers."

After that, we always regarded *café au lait* with a suspicious eye. The expense, however, need not deter those who would use it for a sponge bath, as two quarts amply suffice for this purpose.

The use of natural mineral waters for ablutions must be regarded rather as a means of curing actual disease, than of preserving health. They are all inferior in the latter respect to the water distilled by the sun in the alembic of the clouds, which descends to the earth in refreshing showers.

Sea-bathing is now so fashionable in summer, that we cannot avoid speaking of it from a cosmetic point of view. It is an admirable tonic to the general system, and increases the activity of the circulation and secretion in a marked degree. Thus it often materially improves the looks. Moreover, one of the most important points about it is that at the sea-shore people *will* bathe daily, while at home they *won't*. But as an author of reputation remarks, "As an agent for preserving the softness and delicacy of the healthy skin, and the bright hues of the complexion, it is inferior to the tepid bath." Those who live by the sea are often robust and comely, but rarely have transparent and fine skins.

The tepid bath means one whose temperature is from 80° Fahr. to 90°. When taken daily, one should not as a rule remain in it longer than from three to five minutes, as otherwise it may become debilitating, but once a week the time may be extended to twenty minutes or half an hour, in order to give the whole surface a thorough soaking. Soap need not be used oftener than once or twice a week, unless special circumstances demand it. After the bath, and *always* after washing the face, exposure to the sun or air, especially a cold, damp, raw air, should be avoided for a half hour or hour, as such exposure is apt to spot or chap the skin.

The Turkish bath has been introduced with such a loud blow of trumpets within a few years that we must perforce speak of it at some length. It is a degenerate offspring of the old Roman bath. That luxurious nation had reduced bathing to a system. Establishments for the purpose were found in every city of the Empire, and were of the most splendid and costly construction. Their plan was as follows:—

The first room the guest entered was filled with hot air. Here he remained long enough to break out in a profuse perspiration. Then he was ushered into a large apartment, in the centre of which was a basin of water, heated to about 100° or 105°. In this he soaked, sat, read, and gossiped for a half hour or hour, after which he was led to the next room, and plunged for a moment into cold, clear water. This sudden transition removed the languor left by the previous high temperature, and braced the system for exercise.

16

The clothing was resumed in a moderately warmed room, the body having been previously anointed with fresh olive oil, well rubbed in, to protect it from the action of the air.

The Turkish bath likewise has its hot-air chamber, its hot-water bath, and the moderately heated apartment to dress in; but in Constantinople, and in many establishments in this country, the cold-water douche is lacking. This, however, should never be omitted, as it is important that the system be thus stimulated before going forth into the air.

The value of the Turkish bath depends on the thorough cleansing it gives the system, and on the perspiration it excites. Its peculiar feature is the shampooing process. An expert attendant kneads, rubs, and manipulates every muscle and joint of the body, imparting a suppleness and elasticity to the system very agreeable and often beneficial.

For rheumatics, for those affected with chronic skin diseases, for many complaints, indeed, this bath is admirably suited, and an occasional use of it, say once in ten days or a fortnight, may benefit one who even takes an ordinary bath daily. A more frequent indulgence in health is not advisable.

The Russian bath is said also to be a descendant of old Rome. The bather remains in an apartment filled with either moist or dry air at a very high temperature until in a profuse perspiration, and then adjourns to the next room, and winds up with a plunge into cold water. The peasants, it is said, indulge the national taste in this wise: they have enormous clay stoves in which they sit until thoroughly sweated, and then, naked as they are, rush out of the house and roll in the snow; and this in the midst of a Russian winter, with the thermometer ever so far below zero!

Our own Indians have always been partial to just such a bath. They build a small lodge of skins, heat a number of stones, and pile them in the centre, then, shutting close the apertures, dash water on the stones until the lodge is filled with the hot vapor. After they have enjoyed this a while, they start on a full run for the nearest brook or pond, and plunge in its cool waves. This they look upon as " big medicine," and a specific for all diseases under the sun.

All these methods have the objection that one must breathe the hot air into the lungs. A simple and easy method of taking a Russian bath on a small scale at home, but a method quite as efficient as any other, is this: seat yourself unclothed on a cane-bottomed chair, under which you place a very hot brick on a plate. Wrap a large blanket around you from the neck downward, inclosing the chair, and carefully close the borders. Pour from time to time a little hot water on the brick, and the body will soon be in an atmosphere of highly heated vapor. If a dry-air bath is preferred, place a spirit lamp under the chair, and arrange the blanket as before.   When the perspiration has lasted from fifteen to twenty minutes, throw aside the blanket, and plunge into a tub already filled with cold water, or take a cold shower bath.

The only warning needed in this procedure—but that is an important one—is not to allow the body to become cooled between the hot and the cold stages. The transition must be sudden, and the cold dip or shower must last but for a second or two, otherwise trouble may result.

The effects of frequent and long-continued tepid bathing on the skin is so salutary, that recently Professor Hebra, of Vienna, one of the most celebrated physicians of skin diseases now living—probably we ought to say the most celebrated—has adopted the plan of placing some of his obstinate cases in water up to the neck, and leaving them there for several days! That is, they are tied up in a caoutchouc sack through which a stream of water is constantly flowing.

This is not a novel plan in Europe.   At the mineral springs there, which are celebrated for their virtue in skin diseases, the patients enter the bath, which is a large basin from fifty to a hundred feet square, filled with tepid water to the depth of three feet or so, and remain for hours.   A few years ago we passed some time at the baths of Louéche-les-Bains in Switzerland, in the valley of the Upper Rhone.   Every day we saw from fifty to a hundred guests of both sexes seated on chairs in the bath, with the water reaching about to their armpits. Before them were small tables, on which they played cards or chess, wrote letters, laid their books or needle-work, or else they waded about in groups, talking politics or gossiping. Altogether it formed a curious spectacle. We learned that some remained in the water six or seven hours a day, and the reputation of the springs seems to prove that the results of the method are quite satisfactory.

ON TOILET SOAPS.

Soap-and-water is the burden of the song of most writers on health. We grant the water, but are by no means so enthusiastic about the soap. Many a lady will find her skin softer, whiter, and healthier, by omitting it altogether. The reason is the difficulty in obtaining a perfectly "neutral" soap, that is, one that contains no excess of alkali, and one that has in it no rancid fat globules, injurious oil or coloring matter, or irritating foreign substance.

No one needs to be informed that soaps are made by the action of a powerful alkali, caustic soda, or caustic potash usually, on fat. The cheapest, and consequently the almost universal method, is to do this in the "cold way," instead of by the old process of boiling and "salting out." Unfortunately, the cold way is one of those "cheap and nasty" methods which Carlyle says are becoming daily more popular with this degenerate age. All soap made thus contains an excess of alkali, and particles of fat not saponified. Both these ingredients are harmful to the skin, leaving it rough, tender, and apt to pimple. It is much better to use no soap at all than one which has these injurious qualities.

Toilet soaps should be prepared from clean, sweet tallow or oil by a strong solution of soda, and it is essential that they be completely deprived of an excess of alkali. Their natural color is always a yellow or white, and whatever other hue is given them is artificially done by the admixture of coloring matter.

Brown Windsor is colored by caramel or cacao; rose color is produced by cinnabar, green by chrome-green, and many of the reds by aniline colors. These latter are derived from the distillation of coal oil, and some of them, the fashionable coralline for example, are exceedingly irritating to the skin of many persons, so they should be employed with caution. The dark lines in Castile soap are produced by a preparation of iron, which is harmless.

Any desired perfume can be imparted to soaps, and so long as this is done by the natural odorous portions of the plants, there is no cause of complaint. But most of the toilet soaps sold are perfumed by the artificial essences derived from fusel oil and petroleum, the effects of which upon a delicate skin are occasionally acrid and unpleasant.

Transparent soaps, which are quite popular in most cities, are made by dissolving well-dried tallow soaps in alcohol. Except in appearance, they have no advantage over any other kinds.

Soaps containing sand, pumice-stone, or similar gritty substances, need rarely be used in the toilet. If something of the kind is desired, a piece of pumice stone itself is quite as good. This is a favorite material in the East, where it is employed by the women to polish their nails, and the rough portions of the epidermis.

All this tallow-chandlery talk has not resulted in our fixing on any particular soap. We have, in fact, none to recommend. For bathing purposes, a piece of good white Castile, or of curd soap is as desirable as any. For the hands, a perfumed neutral article may be chosen, not red nor blue, nor too odorous. For the face, the less soap of any sort that is applied to it, the better.

There are a number of medicated soaps in the market stentoriously recommended for curing divers troubles of the skin, and preserving it in a state of perennial beauty. They are generally secret preparations, and when analyzed are found to be the commonest and coarsest soda soaps, perfumed, medicated, and done up in attractive wrappings. They are dangerous to use, and should be shunned.

Not that we would be understood to decry sweepingly the employment of medicated soaps. They are admirable aids in treating skin diseases, as we have repeatedly experienced, but like any other remedial agent, they must be applied with caution, and under advice.

LOTIONS AND WASHES TO BEAUTIFY THE SKIN.

We are now through this talk about soap and water, and can advance directly into the very arcanum of the boudoir, and disclose without delay its most subtle mysteries. Is there any one, perchance, who would care to know a wash that will keep her hands soft, white, and smooth? Is there any belle desirous of preserving her complexion, with its pink and white intact? Are there any who would remove a shining, not to say greasy, appearance of the skin, or a harshness, dryness, and inclination to chap and crack? Let them lend an attentive ear, for we are now about to tell how these ends can be gained.

It is no secret among adepts in the chemistry of the toilet, that certain substances used continuously in a wash have a most excellent effect on the skin, preserving its color and health. But all the adepts like to keep the secret among themselves, and make a trade of their knowledge. We intend to draw the veil from these mysteries, and recommend a number of convenient and efficient preparations, which can be readily compounded in the domestic laboratory, and specify when they are applicable.

Thus, a person who has this shiny, polished complexion, owes it to an unusual secretion of fatty matter by the skin. Soap fails to remove it, and it is altogether better for her to use, instead, a saturated solution of *borax*. Let her wet her face with this, morning and evening, allow it to remain on for several minutes, then wash in rain or filtered water. The philosophy of this is that borax, a mild alkali, unites with the minute globules of fat to form a soap, and thus the face is both cleansed and freed from its greasy appearance.

Such a solution has another delightful result. It prevents the tendency to redness which appears obstinately and annoyingly on the cheeks, nose, and knuckles of some persons. For such ordinary purposes the following recipe is a model one :—

> Take—
>
> | Powdered borax | one half ounce ; |
> | Pure glycerine | one ounce ; |
> | Camphor water | one quart. |

Mix, and use twice a day as directed above. If the camphor water is home-made, filtered rain water must be used. This lotion is better than any sold in the shops for a regular, daily, cosmetic wash. It prevents chapped skin, removes sunburn, keeps the pores in fine condition, and is *cheap*. What more is wanted ? We would not exchange a quart of it for a gallon of the water of the Queen of Hungary, which, in the last century, was the most famous cosmetic lotion in the world.   And what was it ?

Nothing but tincture of rosemary, made with the best brandy and carefully distilled.

The most serene queen Donna Isabella of Hungary, however, set great store by it.   She wrote the receipt for it carefully in her Book of Hours, and added this note : " I, Isabella, Queen of Hungary, when seventy-two years old, gouty and infirm, used a flask of this water, and it had such a wondrous effect that I seemed to grow young and beautiful.   So the King of Poland wished to marry me, and I did not refuse him, out of love to our Lord, who I doubt not sent me this flask by the hands of an angel in the garb of the old hermit from whom I had it."

How many more flasks the old lady used, and how many more husbands she felt in conscience obliged to accept, we have been unable to ascertain.

Some of the very best washes for the complexion can be made of articles which are in every household.   The celebrated Mr. Wilson, of London, recommends constantly in his practice, as of great efficacy in whitening and clearing the skin and complexion of that " muddiness," or shade which is so common, lotions of citric acid.   Now citric acid is simply the acid of lemons, and the following preparation, which any one can make in a few minutes, answers the purpose quite well:—

> Take—
>
> | Fresh lemon-juice | a wineglassful; |
> | Rain water | a pint; |
> | Otto of roses | a few drops. |

Mix, and keep in a well-corked bottle.

The face and hands may be washed with this several times a day, allowing it to remain on three or four minutes before wiping. Whenever there are any superficial and transient stains on the skin not readily removed by soap and water, rubbing the spot with a little piece of lemon should be resorted to next, as in the majority of cases it will quickly remove them.

In France they attribute sovereign cosmetic virtue to the juice of the cucumber. All the shops keep a *lait de concombre*, or a *pommade de concombre*. A German physician of considerable experience also recommends it as an excellent application for preserving the clearness of the complexion. The juice should be pressed from the fruit, brought to the boiling point over a quick fire, cooled rapidly, and securely bottled. A tablespoonful of it diluted with twice the quantity of water may be applied morning and evening.

Another contribution of the kitchen garden to the boudoir is the horse-radish. This is a more useful plant than is generally supposed. The famous botanist Linnæus goes so far as to call it a "divine remedy."

If it can make the fair sex simulate a little more closely to divinities, we shall not think the phrase amiss. An ounce of the fresh root, steeped in a pint of cold buttermilk for four hours, yields a wash which is highly prized in parts of England for removing sunburn, and whitening the skin. The juice pressed out and mixed with twice the quantity of vinegar, has also been recommended for the same purpose, and for removing freckles.

Turning to the apothecary's shelves once more, we take down his jar of *benzoin*. This is a fragrant resin which comes to us from the sunny meadows of Sumatra, and is redolent with odors of the Spice Islands, and the mysterious virtues of tropical balms. Its qualities are strange. Mix a little of it with fat, and the latter will not become rancid. Some of the tincture, combined with glycerine, is simply the best application in the world for chapped hands, and for those sore and cracked nipples which afflict some women so severely during nursing. But this apart. We speak of it now as a cosmetic. Two ounces of it to a pint of pure alcohol (free from acrid fusel oils and the like) make as fine an application as those can ask who wish a white, spotless tint, and fragrant aroma. Some of it may be used once or twice a day in the manner already mentioned.

About a tablespoonful should be poured into a small tumbler of water. It changes the water to a whitish fluid, which is known in France as *lait virginal*, virgin's milk, and is highly and justly esteemed. None of the cosmetic washes is more agreeable. Some glycerine can be added to the water if desired.

We doubt if benzoin is a whit inferior to the Balm of Mecca, or Balm of Gilead, the most famous of all the cosmetic applications of the Orient. So precious and rare is this that it would be dog-cheap at Constantinople at its weight in gold. A pound of the best quality sells there for about fifteen hundred dollars in specie! As for France, England, or America, they get nothing but the refuse.

When Lady Mary Wortley Montague visited Constantinople early in the last century it was more plentiful, and as all her lady friends in Paris and London besieged her for some, she procured several jars of it. On going to bed she rubbed some of it thoroughly on her face. The next morning she woke up with her cheeks red and swollen, "as if she had a dozen toothaches." This alarmed her terribly, but in a few days the swelling disappeared, and all her friends assured her she was vastly improved in looks. She writes, however, in her Letters, that she has no notion of undergoing the ordeal again.

Indeed, the balsam is said to be used only in very minute quantities, and thus applied, may well deserve its reputation, for the Bible itself speaks of it under

17

the name of the "Balm of Gilead" as a medicine of renown in most ancient times.

There are only too many persons in our land whose complexion is "muddied" by a scrofulous taint in their families. They are usually either fair-skinned blondes, or sallow brunettes. Both should make it a rule to employ daily a wash such as this:—

> Take—
>
> | Iodide of potassium | two drachms; |
> | Glycerine | one ounce; |
> | Rain water | one pint. |

Mix them, and apply with a soft sponge.

These are probably enough instructions on this point. Not that the list is nearly exhausted. There are many other excellent cosmetic washes, but they contain such deadly substances as corrosive sublimate, prussic acid, and arsenic, not proper to be used except under the supervision of a physician, and dangerous to keep on the toilet table, where children may reach them. Of such powerful poisons are composed many of the washes sold in the stores, and they should therefore never be ignorantly patronized. Those we have given above are, in most cases, quite as efficient as any, and are all innocuous.

Here we must insert what lawyers call a "proviso" concerning their use. Our readers must remember that we are all this time speaking of a *healthy* skin, and how to keep it. If the skin is already suffering from some local disorder, or if its loss of beauty is owing to the insidious approach of some general malady, then of course these lotions will fail of their effect. Hygiene must then give place to Medicine.

Furthermore, to insure their proper action, not only must the precepts about bathing and exercise, which we have already given, be observed, but especial attention must be paid that the bowels and other organs perform their functions regularly. Without this is looked after, no real improvement can be hoped for from any local remedies whatever. The general health must always be guarded by every one who aspires to prolong the fleeting days of beauty.

EMULSIONS AND POMADES FOR THE SKIN.

Some persons who cannot use soap without experiencing unpleasant sensations, substitute for it various sorts of *emulsions*, as they are called, formed chiefly of ground seeds and nuts which are rich in oil, for example, almonds, cocoanuts, pistachio nuts, etc. These are perfumed to the taste, and can readily be had from leading druggists.

We have already mentioned one of these which can be prepared at home—that made of kernels of English chestnuts, dried and ground into a fine powder. It is quite as good as any. The kernels of bitter-almonds may be used also, but they are poisonous, and therefore objectionable.

Pomades are chiefly used when the skin is harsh or chapped; the most popular is cold-cream. This ought to be made of white wax, pure spermaceti, oil of almonds, and rose-water, with various scents. Some have doubted whether it can be applied for a long time without injury, but the question seems idle. Why should any one apply it for a long time? If it does not correct the trouble soon, throw it aside before it has time to affect the skin, and try something more efficient. Neither it nor any other greasy preparation should be allowed to touch the skin after they have become in the least rancid or altered, as the acrid substances, then present, are certain to mar the softness of the complexion. This rule knows no exceptions.

OTHER MEANS OF IMPROVING THE COMPLEXION.

The noble dames of ancient Rome, who have never been surpassed in luxury, were wont to plaster their faces at night with a poultice of bread-crumbs and asses' milk, which on being removed in the morning left a freshness and whiteness very much prized in their day, and we presume identical with that *teint mat* for which the Italian women of the highest class are still renowned.

They also had recourse to more disagreeable means. Thin slices of fresh meat, veal preferred, were laid on the cheeks and kept there all night. It has been whispered to us that in Paris—we always lay such a scene

in Paris. you know—there are *lionnes* who still have
recourse to this extraordinary procedure to heighten
their charms.   We are obliged to confess that it would
doubtless be efficient, for the albumen in the flesh
would soften the epidermis and loosen its scales.   But
who would be willing to go to such an extreme, when
the object may be attained by cleanlier and more agreeable means?   Or who would follow the example of
Madame Vestris, who, if rumor did not traduce her,
was wont to cover her cheeks and forehead every night,
with what butchers call a "leaf" or "flare," from an
animal freshly killed?

PROTECTING THE COMPLEXION—MASKS AND VEILS.

Sun and air give a ruddy, healthy glow to the face,
but they also roughen and brown it.   They are un-
friendly to the delicate shades of pink and white,
which are the pride or the envy of many a belle.
Therefore from earliest times shields of various sorts
have been devised.

In the Orient and in Spanish countries, women of
the better class rarely go abroad except in thick veils,
with perhaps apertures cut for the eyes.   In Egypt,
the little girls of eight and ten years will find some old
rag to conceal their face from a stranger, though they
leave exposed every inch of the rest of their body.

The custom arose not so much from marital jealousy
and rigid discipline, as from coquetry, and a desire to

guard the complexion against the burning sun and scorching winds of those hot climates. The veil in our more temperate land serves the same purpose. It is an important article of the dress, and should be worn assiduously on going out in a damp and raw, or hot and dry atmosphere. In winter, the sudden change from our furnace-heated houses to the keen outdoor cold is very trying to the skin, and then especially is a thick veil of service. No cook can hope to have a good complexion, or a healthy skin, and it is because she is constantly exposed to just such changes from heat to cold.

Our ancestors were in this respect more careful than we. In the days of the second Charles, and Queen Anne, it was no unusual sight to see ladies in the London thoroughfares wearing masks or half masks, not, as you might suspect, bent on some wild freak, but simply for the purpose of protecting their complexions. In France, the home of coquetry, the usage was already ancient. Margaret of Navarre, queen of Henry IV., she whose wedding torches were quenched in the blood of the massacre of St. Bartholomew, was so in love with her mask that she refused to lay it aside even at night. This irritated her husband, with very good reason, we think, and was the first of a long series of "domestic infelicities." Henry was not choice in his expressions, and roundly said to her no long time after the wedding day:—

" Madam, with that confounded black mask on, you look so much like the devil that I am always tempted to make the sign of the cross to drive you away."

Margaret preferred to lose her husband rather than her complexion, and, when matters went to the extent of suing for a divorce, as they naturally did, Henry offered this nocturnal mask as a grave evidence of conjugal insubordination.

We have already remarked, and we repeat the warning, that exposure to out-door air immediately after washing the hands or face will almost surely change the skin more or less into parchment. The Romans and Greeks knew this, and took care to protect these parts by inunctions of oil; the ladies of the olden time knew it, and covered their faces with their *loups*. If the belles of our own day bore it more constantly in mind, there would be less demand for the artifices by which ruined complexions are concealed. Always, therefore, for at least fifteen minutes after washing the face, remain in a room moderately lighted and moderately warmed. Or if it is necessary to go out, wear a veil, and if the air is raw, rub gently on the skin a few drops of pure glycerine, or dust it with a little rice powder.

WHAT CLOTHING SHOULD BE WORN NEXT THE SKIN?

On a previous page we disavowed any intention of discussing that profound question, the Philosophy of

Clothes, which, according to Mr. Carlyle's favorite hero, Herr Teufeldröck, and (dare we add?) the verdict of many a fair one, simply includes most that is important in this sublunary sphere. Nevertheless, we cannot altogether escape it. It meets us just now in considering how best to protect the skin against outside influences, and we must, perforce, give it attention.

The underclothing—we mean its deepest strata in immediate contiguity to the body—has quite as much to do with a person's comfort, health, and good looks, and consequently with his or her success in life, as the outside apparel, public opinion to the contrary notwithstanding. It is pertinent, here as elsewhere, to look beneath the surface to form our judgment of the individual.

Cleanliness we take for granted. "Foul linen" and healthy skin are incompatibles. Falstaff himself, whose stomach was not easily turned, could not abide the "rank compound of villainous smells" which he suffered in the buck-basket. No excuse, short of that of Queen Isabella, is valid for not changing the underclothing every week. Isabella, daughter of Philip II., wife of the Archduke Albert, swore by the Virgin and all the saints that until her royal husband should reduce the refractory citizens of Ostend, to which he was diligently laying siege, she would not remove a stitch of her clothing.

The stiff-necked burghers proved of doughtier mettle

than she had at all anticipated, and it was three good
years ere her husband could send her word that her
penance was ended, and that she might put on a clean
smock with a clear conscience. By that time, and long
before it, her ruffles and collars had acquired a dingy
brown hue, which out of compliment to her was at once
adopted as the court fashion, under the name of *l'Isa-
beau.*

The first quality demanded in the articles which
come next the skin is, that they be soft and comfortable. They must not irritate, nor be chilly, nor heating. To our mind, one of the most dreadful penances
of convent life is that mentioned by Victor Hugo in
Les Miserables. He says that the nuns of a certain
order are obliged to clothe themselves in harsh woollen
cloth next the skin. The irritation is so distressing
that they are not unfrequently thrown by it into a
fever, and break out in an eruption from head to foot.

The hermits and ascetics of the Middle Ages were
wont to wear shirts of horse-hair cloth. The sharp
ends of the hairs maintained them in that condition of
constant petty misery deemed so salubrious for the
soul. The same condition can nowadays be attained
so easily without this artificial means, that it has fallen
out of vogue.

The amount of clothing should be carefully adjusted
to the temperature. When too scanty, the skin is

chilled and is liable to crack; when too abundant, the excessive warmth may cause an eruption and itchiness.

Cotton, linen, wool, and silk, are the prevailing materials employed. Of these, cotton is the cheapest and commonest. It is a good conductor of heat, and is the best adapted of any of them for warm climates and the hot season. Its fibres, however, are coarser and rougher than those of linen, and there are persons so sensitive to this slight difference, that they cannot wear it. Such must have recourse to linen.

This is notably less irritating. In dressing painful wounds the surgeon always prefers his lint of old linen rather than old cotton rags. But it is not a good conductor, and is therefore less adapted for summer than winter, for a warm climate than a cool one. When removed from the person a short time, and then replaced, as at bathing, it feels chilly and damp, which is much less the case with cotton.

For cold weather, wool or silk is preferable. Both these have one objection. That is, that on the slightest friction they disturb the electricity of the skin, cause a determination of blood to the surface, and sometimes thus lead to cutaneous eruptions. This holds good more particularly against silk, which, in point of texture, is much more agreeable than even the finest wool, and is also a worse conductor of heat The latter is an advantage in winter.

Though this is true, we are decidedly of opinion

that from October to the end of May, in this climate, every person who would guard either health or beauty must wear an ample undergarment of either silk or wool. It may be worn over one of linen if preferred. Many will find it prudent to continue the use of a lighter variety, a merino or silk gauze, through the summer months also.

Even the *color* of the garment next the skin must not be overlooked. There is a time-honored notion, familiar to every one, that *red* flannel has some peculiar virtue about it. The old women recommend it for "rheumatiz" and "stiff joints." However well-founded this venerable prepossession may have been in the good old times when the dye-stuffs were derived from vegetable extracts, we regret that we must throw discredit on it at present. Many of the reds now employed in the arts are obtained from coal-oil and from the salts of mercury, both of which contain acrid and poisonous principles. Within a year or two a number of cases have been reported, where painful cutaneous diseases arose from wearing articles thus dyed.

One young gentleman, mentioned by Dr. Tardieu of Paris, who seemed to fancy, with Sir Andrew Ague-cheek, that his leg "looked indifferent well in a flame-colored stock," sent in haste for his physician the next morning after wearing a pair. Precisely so far as the red hose had extended, there was a marked inflammation of the skin.

Any decided color should be rejected. Our recommendation is to avoid all dyed garments whatever next the skin, and if we *do* yield to the charms of delicate flesh tints in gloves and stockings, it is with some disturbance of our professional conscience. Skin gloves, be it remembered, dyed on the outer side, do not come within the ban.

POWDERS TO PROTECT THE SKIN.

We hardly know whether to call powder a legitimate aid to the toilet in health, or not. But, on mature reflection, we venture to do so. Every mother knows how essential it is, in the care of infants, to prevent chafing and cracking. Many retain this same cutaneous delicacy all their lives, and for such, a good toilet powder is a necessity.

Its use might with propriety be extended. Many a woman would be improved if she were to dust a little over the surface after every bath and every ablution. Dr. Veron, in his *Mémoires*, tells an incident which aptly illustrates its preservative effects.

"I know a woman," says the old *bourgeois de Paris*, "of some sixty years, whose physiognomy is remarkable. Her gray hairs betray her age, but there is not the least wrinkle upon her face. This woman has told me her secret. It is this: All her life she has had recourse to the most frequent ablutions. In the morning, in the evening, and whenever chagrin had loosened her tears, every few hours she bathed her face, and dusted it by throwing over it a light cloud of rice-powder."

We have already spoken a word in favor of powder after ablutions, *apropos* of Anne Boleyn. It should be kept for this purpose in a fine gauze bag, with which the surface can be lightly tapped, or the swan's-down brush may be chosen. After thus depositing on the surface a thin film, all loose particles should be gently brushed away. An invisible stratum will then remain, protecting the skin from noxious influences.

But everything depends on having a powder which will itself be perfectly innoxious. Here, as elsewhere, we shall follow our plan of giving receipts for several quite as effective, much cheaper, and by all odds safer than many of those whose ingredients are unknown, and whose only merit is their elegant wrappers.

For ordinary toilet purposes, none is superior to that commonly used in the nursery, which is nothing but very finely-powdered starch (that from arrowroot is the best), scented with orris-root and essences. The rice powder, *poudre de riz*, mentioned in the extract from Dr. Veron we have just given, is very finely ground rice-meal, scented to the taste.

When there is any chafed surface on the person, in the flexures of the joints or elsewhere, one-fourth the

18

quantity of lycopodium can be added to the starch powder with great benefit.

So far as a simple powder is concerned, the one we have now given is sufficient, but there is another use for which these preparations are demanded, somewhat more ambitious. It is to whiten the skin, to lend a hue to the surface which nature has withheld, or taken back.

This brings us at once to the second part of our subject, that in which we proposed to treat of those cosmetic arts, invented to hide the victories which Time has already won. Not to waste space in prefatory remarks, we commence at once with:—

MEANS FOR WHITENING THE SKIN.

These are numerous enough to allow considerable liberty of choice. That which we are inclined to name first as preferable to the others, is *powdered French chalk.* This is, in fact, not chalk at all, but a fine variety of soapstone, obtained at Briançon, a small village in the French Alps, and therefore known in commerce as *craie de Briançon.* It is very fine, very white, and very adhesive. It does not injure the skin in the least, and does not lose it color by the secretions of the body, nor by exposure to coal-gases, or sunlight.

As the pure Briançon stone is not always to be had, we have taken the pains to examine specimens from most of the soapstone quarries in the United States, and after considerable search we found an article, in every way equal to the very best imported. This is from the mountain region of North Carolina, and is ground and sold for various purposes by a Cincinnati firm. We have called their attention to its value as a cosmetic, and it richly deserves to take the place of the long-celebrated *craie de Briançon.*

Venetian chalk, so-called, is not a chalk either, but talc. It is inferior to the French both in color and adhesive power. In order to whiten it, the manufacturer exposes it to a high heat. This improves its color, but diminishes its adhesive qualities.

Another substance, said to be an especial favorite in some portions of our country, is finely-powdered, light carbonate of magnesia. This is also harmless, but is in other respects inferior to the French chalk.

All these powders have the objection that the hue they produce is not a very decided and brilliant one. Therefore the *cosmetiqueur,* with daring hands, has invaded the domain of pharmacy, and laying hold of some of its most potent and dangerous drugs has carried them to his shop to sell to the first chance-comer. This is unwise, and many a tolerable complexion has been wizened into a piece of parchment, many a woman has poisoned her constitution, by ignorantly using these perilous stuffs.

We do not say that all are injurious. We must

exercise discrimination. One of the favorite articles, the only one which will produce that *teint mat*, which we have previously described, as almost monopolized by the noble ladies of Italy, who hardly ever see the sun, and which was all the rage at Paris a year or so ago, is *bismuth*. The apothecary sells it under the name of "pearl powder," "pearl white," and "bismuthine cream." Several forms of the mineral are used, but most commonly the subnitrate, though the famous French cosmetic *fard blanc de bismuth*, is what chemists call a subchloride.

Some physicians have decried this metal in both these forms as injurious to the skin and unsafe to the general health. There is doubt about this opinion. We have given it for months, both internally and externally, without any ill results, and do not feel convinced that it is more objectionable on the score of health than French chalk. It has, indeed, in common with *all* the metallic substances used for this purpose, one serious drawback. They are all changed by sulphurous gases into dark gray sulphurets, and as luck will have it, our coal fires and gas-pipes are constantly ready, whenever opportunity is allowed them, to fill the apartment with just such gases. The consequence is that on not a few occasions, ladies, who at the outset of the evening displayed complexions which made their rivals ready to tear their hair with envy, have come to grief in the most unexpected manner, and been obliged to retire in confusion, with their faces of a dirty ash color, owing to some stupid servant mismanaging the furnace and allowing the gas to escape.

Another metallic substance, which makes a fine white and is quite harmless, and, indeed, if moderately used, actually beneficial to the skin, is *precipitated carbonate of zinc.* It is a favorite application in skin diseases, and when parts are chafed, or have slight eruptions, its use will be found healing as well as beautifying. There is no objection to applying it to the most delicate portions, such as the edges of the eyelids, or the nipples when they are tender. With an equal amount of French chalk, it forms a powder highly extolled by some excellent authorities.

If the ambition of beauty had stopped here, we should have had no complaint to make. But no! a more decided color is demanded, a more brilliant tint than nature herself ever grants. To obtain this, recourse is had to those unwholesome metals, lead and mercury. These, in the form of carbonate of lead or flake white, and the mercurial white precipitate, have been, and still are vended for the purpose. They are certain to destroy both beauty and health, and the woman who uses them may think herself lucky if her life too is not imperilled. Moreover, when used, they give as we have said a hue so brilliant, that any observer can see that it is unnatural. Therefore, from a cosmetic as well as a hygienic point of view, they must be condemned, for the perfection of art is to achieve an absolute resemblance to nature at her best, not to surpass her, nor fall behind her.

ROSE-POWDERS AND ROUGE.

At the very name of rouge we suppose that many women—no, we won't say many, but some—will throw up their hands in horror. They associate it, innocent lambs, only with the bedaubed creatures who pace the pavements at night, with Jezebels "who paint themselves," and with actresses who stand before the footlights, reddened up to the eyes.

We, who know more intimately this progressive land of ours, cannot but smile at such notions. Any fashionable apothecary of our great cities can rehearse a long list of customers very different from these. The occasional use of such artificial coloring is common, and such being the case, however much we may disapprove of it, persons should know something about the materials from which it is prepared, and be placed on their guard against dangerous combinations.

Rose-powders, or flesh-colored powders, are prepared from any of the white powders we have mentioned by adding to them a little carmine and ochre until the desired tint is obtained. The soap-stone powder, thus tinged with the purest carmine, yields one of the best hues, and is harmless.

But the most fashionable, popular, and easiest means to imitate the glow on the cheek of youth is—*rouge.*

The word *rouge* in French simply means *red*, and is applied to a great variety of products having this color. That, however, which is put up and sold for the complexion is generally, and should be always, derived from one of two sources: either from cochineal, a small bug found on the leaves of the cactus plant in Brazil, which yields *carmine*, or from the familiar plant known as "dyer's saffron," or safflower, which furnishes *carthamine.* The latter is called *rouge végétale.* A cheap, inferior, and injurious article is prepared from vermilion, which is a form of mercury, and should be avoided.

The preparation of rouge is one of the most delicate operations in practical chemistry, and hardly any but the French have succeeded in producing a first class article. There is reason for this beyond mere technical skill, as a London manufacturer once learned to his cost. He had tried repeatedly to equal the French article, and failed just as often. In despair, he visited one of the most famous houses of Lyons, and offered the principal thirty thousand francs if he would show him their process. The principal accepted, and conducted the Englishman through the establishment. What was the disappointment of the latter to find the methods in every respect identical with his own. He returned home, tried again, and failed again. The principal of the Lyons house invited him once more, and put the inquiry:—

"What was the state of the weather when you made the experiment?"

"The weather!" replied the Englishman, "the weather! I don't remember. What has that to do with it?"

"Everything," replied the principal. "It is only on the fairest days in this favored climate, that we can make our carmine."

"If that's your secret," said the visitor, "I had better have kept my thirty thousand francs, as it will do me little good in the London fogs."

There are numerous forms in which rouge is applied. The simplest is "rose powder," which is merely the finest rice meal, tinged with carmine, and perfumed with oil of roses, or some other scent. What is called "enamel powder" is a mixture of equal parts of bismuth (pearl-white) and French chalk (soapstone), colored and scented in the same manner. Either of these is harmless, for neither carmine nor carthamine has any injurious action on the skin.

When rouge is sold by itself, it comes in shallow pots or saucers, *rose en tasse*, in pomade, *en crêpons*, or *en feuilles*. The *crêpons* are pieces of silk or cotton gauze, twisted into the shape of a plug, and imbued with the coloring matter (*carthamine*.) Some of them are mounted on wooden or ivory handles, and are then

called *tampons au rouge.* The manner of using them
is to moisten them with alcohol, and rub them gently
on the cheeks or lips. The leaf rouge, *rouge en
feuilles*, is a very elegant preparation. It is usually
prepared by depositing a thin layer of the finest carmine on thick paper. The surface of the paper is to be
moistened by a woollen rag or soft sponge, and gently
rubbed on the skin. The effect is altogether satisfactory.

It is more prudent to use these preparations than
those numberless ones sold under attractive names,
about which nothing is known. One of these, which
has a wide popularity, is a solution of carmine in rose-
water with the addition of strong caustic ammonia,
which latter cannot fail but injure the skin in time.
Above all things, beware of *cheap* rouges, and those
called "theatre rouges," nearly all of which are coarse
colors which give a tawdry and meretricious air to the
user, and besides that are generally made of vermilion.

There has recently been introduced into the market,
under the outlandish name of *schnouda*, and the more
romantic one of "Sympathetic Blush," a very curious
coloring for the skin, which is asserted to surpass all
others in its absolute resemblance to the roseate hue
of health. What is not the least singular about it is
that it is perfectly colorless itself, and remains so until
it has been some minutes on the surface. It is prepared by mixing with cold-cream a small proportion of

alloxan, one of those newly-discovered combinations, the source of which we hesitate to explain. This undergoes a chemical alteration when brought in contact with the skin, and produces a strikingly natural pink hue. Whether or not it is as innocent as the rouges we have described, is as yet unknown.

When the inventive genius of the boudoir had in this manner prepared materials for whitening, and again for reddening the skin, it had not yet completed its task. There still remained the blue lines of the veins, which course beneath the skin, and unless something was found to include these in the " make up," the art were sadly at fault.

It has been done. The elegant world can now provide itself with little jars which contain finely-powdered French or Venetian chalk, made into a paste with gum-water, colored to the proper tint with Prussian blue, and accompanied with little leather pencils, all manufactured on purpose to portray with anatomical fidelity the direction and hue of the veins. The effect, says Professor Hirzel, who talks on this subject with the gusto of a connoisseur, " when the work is artistically performed, is good and natural."

A WORD ABOUT " ENAMELLING" THE FACE.

There has been such a noise in the newspapers of recent years about " enamelling" the face, that we are in duty bound to say a word about it. The most absurd stories are afloat. One we noticed asserted that the late actress, Madame Vestris, was obliged to sit " hours" by the fire to allow her " enamel" to dry. Another stated that certain New York belles visit Paris annually to have their complexions " made up" for the year. An enterprising rascal, taking advantage of popular credulity, advertises in various papers to enamel faces " to last a day or a year."

Such paragraphs arise from ignorance. The so-called method of " enamelling" is simply painting the face, and for this purpose the artists always prefer the poisonous salts of lead, as they yield much more striking effects. Practice often gives these persons a decided skill in their specialty, but their customers pay for it doubly, first in money and then in health.

The skin is usually prepared by an alkaline wash, wrinkles and depressions are filled with a yielding paste, and the colors are laid on to the requisite extent, first the white and then the red.

No such procedure can give a durable covering to the face, and no one should submit herself to the hands of the ignorant and unscrupulous parties who choose this for a business. The simple and harmless means which we have explained will suffice, if skilfully used, to conceal the ravages of years to any proper extent.

PATCHES—AN HISTORICAL REMINISCENCE.

Antiquaries have puzzled themselves to explain the
origin of patches. They could not understand why a
woman with brilliant complexion would, as they
thought, disfigure herself with little pieces of black
plaster on her face. They did not remember, these
simple antiquaries, that if we wish to set off in bold
relief a white object, we place it on a black ground. It
was not imitation of some noble dame who concealed a
pimple with a plaster, but a coquetry founded on the
law of contrasting colors, which introduced patches.
Like other fashions, they

> "Come, and pass, and turn again."

Hints of them are scattered in classical lore, Anglo-
Saxon monks saw their revival, and the gossipy Pepys
witnessed their introduction at the Court of Charles
II., and though he found it difficult, at first, to partake
of Mrs. Pepys' enthusiasm for them, in a few months
we find him not only reconciled to the novelty, but
quite warm in its praise. A century later, Le Camus
defines at length, with curious criticism, the varying
expressions which the patch worn in different parts of
the face gives to the wearer. He tells us that in his
day they were diverse in figure, crescents, stars, crosses,
etc.

Another century has gone by, and once more the
patch seems to be coming into favor. The newspapers

have started a violent opposition to it, and may check or suppress it. But after all, the fashion is a harmless one, and is not irrational. As we have said, it is founded on acknowledged laws of taste, and nothing from a hygienic point of view is to be urged against it. We do not plead for it, but what ground is there for a philippic against it?

DISCOLORATIONS OF THE SKIN.

Leaving these cosmetic arts, which we may call the "tricks of the trade," we pass on to cosmetic science, which occupies itself with the nobler study of remedying and removing those defects which the arts only seek to conceal.

An important branch of it is that which treats of the various discolorations of the skin, all of which detract more or less from beauty. They are well nigh as numerous as the colors of the spectrum, and are of very diverse origin. It may be said of them as Malvolio says of greatness: "Some are born great, some achieve greatness, and some have greatness thrust upon them." So some of these beauty-blemishes are born with persons, others are acquired by want of care, and others are forced upon the most careful.

Some of them are peculiar to certain periods of life and physical conditions. Brown patches not unfrequently arise during pregnancy, and disappear after confinement. A red flush, temporary in character, oc-

19

casionally marks the change of life. Pallor and slight blueness are sometimes recurrent with the periodical illness. Such discolorations cannot be amended, and the best that can be done is to conceal them when social life requires it.

Another large class are characteristic of disease, and can only be removed by a judiciously regulated and often protracted course of treatment. Here the family physician should be called in, who, if he is a wise man, will not depreciate the importance of even so small a sign as an altered complexion, for this is sometimes the only sign and forerunner of serious maladies.

" The green sickness," so common in young girls, derives its name from the peculiar greenish hue of the complexion. Another not less familiar complaint is jaundice, in which the skin takes on a sickly yellow. In a less degree, this same tint is frequently perceptible in persons who are "bilious," or who suffer from dyspepsia. A light bluish hue, most strongly marked on the lips, often betrays disease or defective action of the heart, the seat of life. A lead-colored tinge points to disease of the spleen.

There is a rare complaint named after Dr. Addison, who first explained it, in which the whole surface of the body gradually changes to a tawny brown or mahogany color; and another, not so rare, which indeed is not infrequent, where dark red spots appear in great numbers under the skin, and hence it is called in medical Latin *purpura*, the purples.

In any of these maladies, it is worse than useless for persons without medical education to undertake their own cases. We mention them as those in which we shall *not* suggest home treatment. They demand the services of the professional healer, and are beyond the reach of cosmetic art. Life itself is threatened. But there are many smaller troubles which imperil the charms, for which every woman can be her own prescriber, and these we shall proceed to inform her about.

EXCESSIVE WHITENESS OR PALENESS OF THE SKIN.

A white skin is a boon of Venus, but pallor we associate with sickness and debility, which are nowise akin to personal beauty. It is just as easy for the skin to be too white, as too red or too brown.

Some are troubled with this paleness from childhood, in others it results from failing health. In both cases the blood is at fault. It demands more carbon to form pigment, more iron wherewith to fabricate in nature's wondrous laboratory, the roses that bloom in the cheeks of beauty. For, strange as it may seem, it is these familiar and homely substances, charcoal and iron, which the magic wand of Nature transforms into delicate dyes, and spreads out on the satin skin

of the brunette, or mixes in the crimson current to
produce the mantling blush, the ruby lip, and the—

> " Streaks of red that mingle there,
> Such as are on a Catherine pear,
> The side that 's next the sun."

But it is not enough to adopt such a diet, or to
commence a course of such medicines as shall introduce
into the system these indispensable materials in the
form best adapted to be readily taken up by the blood.
This is, indeed, essential, but, beyond this, the surface
of the body must be stimulated by regular and prolonged frictions.

We all know that if we rub a part it will soon become red.   This is because the minute bloodvessels in
the true skin are brought into increased activity, and
carry a larger amount of the crimson fluid. Let them frequently be so excited, and this habit will become their
nature, and a permanent florid hue will result.   There
is no need to explain with what advantage we can apply
what we learn from this simple fact to the improvement
of the looks, nor to dilate on the value of friction when
it is so readily perceived.

Still another step must be taken, and this for most
people the hardest of all. Professor MaxMüller, the
philologist, has a favorite theory that the degeneration of languages is owing to the universal laziness
of the human race. People are too indolent to pronounce the whole of a word or phrase, so they clip it to

the briefest dimensions; as, for example, when in conversation we catch ourselves saying, "I'd 'a bought it," for "I would have bought it." So, in another sphere, physicians notice that if a medicine is prescribed, it is gulped with alacrity; if a diet is ordered, it is observed with no inordinate grumbling; but when it comes to *exercise*, regular, vigorous, daily exercise, it is the hardest task in the world to persuade any body to take it.

Yet it is this which is so essential to increase the rapidity and volume of the circulation, to aid the digestion, to give roundness to the form, and to dash the blood in rapid and ruddy waves, seventy, eighty, ninety a minute, all over the body. If the local circulation of the skin is increased by friction, so must the general circulation be improved by regular exercise.

Let us sum up in a few words the prescription for those who, without suffering from any disease, are yet disfigured by a colorless skin, pale lips, and a general want of red blood: A diet, or dose, or both, well supplied with carbon and iron, a lukewarm bath (75° to 85°) every morning, followed by thorough friction with a rough towel, active exercise in the sun and air, and the avoidance of alkaline and astringent soaps and washes.

"But the diet—what diet do you mean? How are we to eat charcoal and iron—dirty things?"

Not, certainly, in the shape of soot or spikes, but as

palatably done up by that apothecary-in-chief, Organic
Nature, in familiar articles of food.

As for the iron, if any one would make a first-class
ferruginous tonic, he cannot do better than take a
gallon of hard cider, and throw into it a couple of hand-
fuls of the scales, which the brawny arm of the black-
smith scatters from his red-hot bars in starry showers.
A small wineglassful of this before each meal will work
wonders.

Besides the friction we have mentioned as a stimulant to the skin, and which is not well borne by every
one, there is another resource—electricity. The use
of this agent in medicine is becoming more and more
extended every year, and in its different forms, its
value as a cosmetic is very great. One of the simplest
means of applying it is to wear silk next the skin. As
we have already said, any friction then disturbs the
electrical condition of the skin, and produces a flush.
If the battery is used, brushes made for the purpose
are passed rapidly over the surface, causing a not unpleasant tickling sensation, and bringing the blood to
the minute vessels with marked force. That method
which is called "general electrization," is especially
applicable to cases such as we have been describing.

General paleness, we have said, is hardly a disease,
as many persons have it all their lives, and seem to
enjoy good health. But when a limited portion of the
skin becomes much whiter than the rest, and especially

when it is a dull or a glossy white, then there is some actual mischief going on. Such spots not unfrequently occur on the hands and face, remaining stationary for years, and giving no uneasiness except what is mental.

They are allied to that singular bleaching of color which makes "albinoes" in the colored races. Everyone who has seen many negroes has observed some with these white spots on them. They arise from a want of coloring matter in the skin, and are not easily effaced. What is needed, is to stimulate the little cells beneath the epidermis to take up the coloring matter in the blood, as is their duty. To accomplish this, thorough and repeated electrization is one of the best agents. Or the spots may be frequently rubbed with a tincture prepared by pouring spirits of camphor on red peppers. Or, this failing, a small quantity of the following ointment, highly extolled by a distinguished French surgeon, may be rubbed in three times a day:—

Take

Tannic acid	two scruples;
Fresh lard	one ounce;
Otto of roses	two drops.

Mix, and see that it is preserved from rancidity.

Leprosy is a disease of terrible renown which is characterized by a dead-white skin. The leper is still a dreaded object, banished from the family and shunned in the street, in Oriental countries. The disease is contagious, and next to incurable. Even a shake of the hand is enough to convey it. If it were more prevalent in this country, we would adduce this as another reason why this nuisance of promiscuous hand-shaking should be suppressed. Fortunately, it is extremely uncommon, and when met with is apparently not communicable.

The disfigurement is, however, permanent and distinct. In the instance of one young married lady, with whom we were acquainted, the excessive whiteness was modified by long-continued small doses of nitrate of silver, which gives the skin a bluish or violet tint, not desirable, indeed, but in her opinion preferable to the leprous chalkiness.

This effect of nitrate of silver or lunar caustic, as it is familiarly termed, is certain to follow its long-continued use. But as its consideration does not come under the present heading, we must commence a new section under the title

DISCOLORATIONS FROM NITRATE OF SILVER.

When these result from merely handling a stick or a solution of lunar caustic, they should be washed in a solution of iodide of potassium, which will change them from a brown to a dead white, and then removed by a solution of ammonia (spirits of hartshorn).

But when, as just mentioned, the whole body has a violet or blue tinge, the question is more serious. Unfortunately, some years ago, the nitrate obtained quite a reputation for curing epilepsy, and though it rarely answered the expectations of physicians and patients, it was administered and continued for a long time in a large number of cases. Moreover, most of the hair dyes which are vended for imparting a "glossy black," or a "lustrous brown," contain this powerful ingredient in considerable quantities, and several cases are on record where ladies, who freely used such nostrums, finished by obtaining the coveted color not only on their hair, but on the whole body. From these causes, there are many persons living who carry on their hands and faces the lasting imprint of this drug.

This is as much as saying that any ready means of removal is not known. Such, in fact, is the case, but still there are instances on record where a successful result is asserted to have been obtained by a persevering use of dilute nitric acid internally, and frequent ablutions in water containing iodide of potassium.

SUNBURN, TAN, AND FRECKLES.

The sun is no friend of a dainty visage. The belles of yore knew this, and jealously guarded their charms from its rays, lest they should become, like Cleopatra,

" With Phœbus' amorous pinches, black."

"The stupid sun;" said a great lady of the days of le Grande Monarque, "all it does is to spoil beauty and show ugliness!"

Now-a-days, we are content to parry its attacks with

parasols, veils, and "sundowns." These are sufficient in our more active lives, and we may well dispense with the masks, the closed and darkened carriages, and the sombre rooms, in which those pampered dames indulged. Then, too, perhaps we have means to remove the traces of exposure more rapidly than they.

Sunburn, no one needs to be informed, is the redness which remains on the skin after exposure to high heat. The skin peels off, and the surface is hot, inflamed, and tender. It may be produced by the sun, or the same effect may follow sitting too near a hot fire, or from bending over a brazier or a stove. Those who cherish a delicate complexion should never sit too near the fire or the flue. When the exposure is only occasional, we can readily remove it, but when frequently repeated, it is extremely intractable. For an occasional sunburn, the following pomade is really good. It may be applied at night after washing the skin, and be allowed to remain until morning. It not only lessens the redness, but soothes the burning, dry, and irritated feeling of the skin:—

    Take—

Spermaceti	two ounces ;
Oil of almond	two ounces ;
Honey	one teaspoonful ;
Otto of roses (or any scent)	a few drops.

Melt the spermaceti in a pipkin, then add the oil of almonds, and when they are thoroughly mixed, stir in the honey. Take the pipkin off the fire, and stir constantly until it is cool, adding the scent.

Another most excellent preparation for the same purpose, which contains a portion of that valuable cosmetic, gum benzoin, is what is known in pharmacy as the benzoinated oxide of zinc ointment, with the addition of two drachms of strong spirits of camphor to the ounce. It should be applied in the same manner as the last. One or the other of these will often by a single application relieve the disagreeable sensation, and after a few nights disperse the disfiguring redness. When neither is at hand, the face should be smeared with cold cream—not the artificial but the natural article—on retiring to bed. It often answers very well.

Some persons burn red much easier than others, and it is popularly regarded and with justice, as a sign of good health. The same difference in individuals is observable in *tan*. This is the brown discoloration rapidly produced on some skins by the solar rays. Here as elsewhere, the dark hue is owing to a minute layer of carbon which is deposited on the under surface of the epidermis. There are many recipes given for removing tan. Washing the hands frequently in buttermilk is a domestic suggestion, which proves satisfactory after a day or two. Or vinegar in which fresh-grated horse-radish has been soaked, may be rubbed over the skin. Lemon-juice, too, has its advocates.

A quicker procedure is to dissolve magnesia in clean rain water, beat it to a thick mass, spread it on the face, and let it remain for two or three minutes. Then wash it off with Castile soap and tepid soft water, and rinse thoroughly.

A thin plaster spread with tartaric acid also acts efficiently and promptly.

The solutions of corrosive sublimate, and other powerful agents, used by some persons are altogether too dangerous to form part of a lady's toilet washes under ordinary circumstances. They may fall into the hands of children, and destroy their lives. Moreover, while their cosmetic value is indisputable when judiciously employed, we have known some cases where extremely weak solutions—much milder than ordinarily used—have caused violent and painful eruptions. We leave them then among those agents only to be employed under the eye of the physician.

Freckles are likewise the marks of Apollo's kisses. Many a fine skin is spotted over with them on the first exposure to the winds of March, and its vernal sun. They remain during the summer, and nearly or quite disappear in winter. Others have them all the year. They, too, are deposits of carbon beneath the scarf-skin. Place some blistering fluid over one, and the scarf-skin will come away, and the freckle with it.

This is a severe method of treating them. It is paying dear for one's good looks. In fact, as one might suppose from the number of persons disfigured with them, it is by no means easy to suggest an effectual remedy for freckles. Nearly all the means which are proposed in the books are powerful caustics, which destroy the scarf-skin. They succeed for a time, but with the return of the epidermis the freckle returns also.

A simple, harmless, and occasionally quite successful wash is a saturated solution of borax in rose-water. It should be applied five or six times a day, and allowed to dry upon the skin.

The following formula enjoys some celebrity, and can readily be compounded at home:—

> Take—
> Best English mustard in
>   powder   a tablespoonful;
> Lemon juice   enough to make a thick paste;
> Oil of almonds   a teaspoonful.

Mix them well, and apply, spread in a thin plaster, night and morning until the skin smarts. After a few days, the scarf-skin should loosen and the freckles disappear. After they have gone, the surface should be washed several times daily with a solution of borax.

After the skin has been softened by some almond paste, or a light poultice, lemon-juice will sometimes be successful in removing freckles. A freshly-cut lemon may be rubbed on the spot.

20

Dr. Savignac recommends strongly lotions of Vichy water, night and morning, continued for several minutes, and allowed to dry without wiping. This can certainly do no harm.

LIVER-SPOTS AND MOLES.

An ugly brown patch with distinct outlines sometimes appears on the face, and especially the forehead, at or just below the line of the hair. This is called in common language a "liver-spot." Writers on skin diseases give it a dozen names, so it is useless to mention any of them.

These blotches differ in size, shape, and position, but have an aggravating similarity in being all very ruinous to beauty, and very obstinate in remaining. We have seen them much more frequently in the Mississippi valley than in the Atlantic States, and have been told by others of experience that the ladies of Chicago, Milwaukee, and St. Louis, are more liable to them than those of New York and Boston. It may be that the greater dryness of the interior has something to do with this, if it be true.

Though called "liver-spots," they have not always to do with the liver. They rarely show the yellow tinge which characterizes the deposits of bile. Very frequently, however, they arise from some derangement of this or some other organ, and it is useless to attempt their removal until this derangement is set aside. Either it is the liver that is torpid, enlarged, or diseased, or there is dyspepsia, or some malady or irregularity peculiar to women, or, what is perhaps as common a cause as any, there are internal piles.

Nothing local need be attempted until the general health is thoroughly cared for. Then, with a fair prospect of success, we may proceed to treat the spot itself. This is to be done in the following manner: Rub the whole of the spot, but none of the skin beyond its border, at night with this pomatum:—

| Elder-flower ointment | one ounce ; |
| Sulphate of zinc | twenty grains. |

Leave it on till morning, then wash it away with white Castile soap and soft water, and bathe the part repeatedly with the following lotion:—

| Citric acid | thirty grains ; |
| Infusion of roses | half a pint. |

After the spot has disappeared, which, if the treatment succeeds, will be within a fortnight, the borax and glycerine, or the iodide of potash lotion, should be regularly used, so as to prevent its return.

This is as efficacious a treatment for liver-spots as can be carried out by a person not familiar with drugs. There is another, in which a strong mercurial and resin plaster is laid on the spot at night, and oxymel of squills rubbed in during the day, which has been praised by many as of certain effect (the health being good) within eight days. But this is a somewhat severe procedure, and would not do to recommend for domestic practice.

Washes of chlorine and chloride of lime, which are often suggested for these discolorations, should be employed cautiously. Even when they do disperse the coloring matter, they nearly always leave the skin of a grayish cast, and seamed with fine wrinkles.

It is only rarely that after any of these "heroic" remedies, as physicians call them, those, we mean, which act violently on the epidermis, the patient can hope for a transparent and handsome skin. The brownness disappears, but a whiteness takes its place, owing to a thickening of the scarf-skin. This is not very noticeable, and is in every respect to be preferred to the blotch, but the fact that such will generally be the result of even the most judicious treatment may as well be known at the outset.

The brown spots called *moles* are usually brought with us from birth. They deserve no attention except where they are on some conspicuous portion of the body, and thus interfere with comeliness. Some of them are on a level with the neighboring healthy skin, others slightly prominent, and both varieties are apt to be studded with long, coarse hairs. In former ages, when patches were in vogue, they could readily be concealed, or cherished as a natural patch, a "beauty spot," as they are still sometimes called. Now that we

cannot utilize them in this way, it is best to remove
them entirely. If they are small, this can promptly be
done by a surgeon with caustic or the knife, but if
large, they must be treated in the same manner as
other "mothers' marks," as we shall now proceed to
explain.

MOTHERS' MARKS.

Some of these, such as the absence of members and
deformities, do not come under our present consideration. We shall speak only of those which are upon
the skin, usually coloring it a bright red, a brown, or
a purple. It has been estimated that one person in
each thousand has some spot of this nature on the
parts of the body usually exposed. They are known
as strawberry, cherry, or raspberry marks, and are
caused by an enlargement of the minute bloodvessels
in the derma, or true skin.

To remove them, we must destroy these minute vessels,
or cause them to shrivel and diminish to their natural
size. In some few cases, this can be done by tying
the artery which supplies them with blood. Generally
this is impossible. Again, there are certain substances
which are supposed to act specifically on the cutaneous
veins, paralyzing and constricting them. One of these
is ergot, another, one of the preparations of bismuth.
The scarf-skin can be removed by a blister, and plasters

containing these substances applied.   This is painful and only succeeds in mild cases.

Many years ago two French surgeons, MM. Lepeyre and Lecomte, observed that the rays of the sun, concentrated by a lens or burning-glass, exert a peculiar and propitious effect on certain cutaneous diseases. The chemical properties of sunlight, they thought, must have something to do with this, and they called the attention of the profession to their observations.   Like many other useful discoveries, however, the process was suffered to lapse almost into forgetfulness.   Within the past few years it has been revived, chiefly by the exertions of a person not a member of the profession, and even more has been claimed for it than it is rightfully entitled to.

There is no doubt but that it is the most efficacious means yet devised to destroy these red birth-marks, but it requires no little practice and judgment to obtain favorable results.   The heat must be so adjusted as to shrivel the vessels in the true skin without destroying the skin itself, as otherwise a scar will result.   We have employed these glasses in several instances, and are convinced that they are a most important addition to our means to combat these trying disfigurements.

INDIA-INK OR TATTOO MARKS.

Girls are wiser than boys.

If we want a proof of it, see how many urchins mar

their hands and arms for life, by pricking into the
skin some design with India-ink, or with gunpowder
dissolved in water. It can never be erased, an.
though in after years they would not grudge a purse
of broad pieces to have this brand wiped away, it cannot be done.

Were it with some yellow, red, or green dye, it
might be neutralized by introducing a decolorizing
substance, but with India ink, gunpowder, carbon—
never.

We heard of one unfortunate lad, whose companions
in jest seized him and tattooed a star on the end of
his nose! What an affliction it must have been to him
all his life!

Girls are too sensible to indulge in such improper
freaks. Perhaps not one in a million, be she ever so
wild and thoughtless, would thus go to work to spoil
her beauty. Sailors and soldiers, on the other hand,
delight in covering their skin with these ineffaceable
emblems. Some inscribe their names, others the
emblems of their business, or the face of their lady-love.
Many a one lives to regret it.

When Jules Bernadotte, son of a provincial attorney
at Pau, was sergeant-major in the French revolution,
he was a radical republican. He then pricked into
the back of his hand the emblems of the French Republic, which was to be immortal. But when the
Republic was ingloriously defunct, and Jules Berna-

dotte was no longer sergeant-major, but was Charles XIV., King of Sweden, the republican emblems on his hand were beyond all expression annoying, and *mal apropos*. If a man ever wished to rid himself of such a brand, Bernadotte did. As he was rich, powerful, and a king, he succeeded. The same method, we are glad to add, can be applied to one who is neither of these. We shall relate it.

An ingenious surgeon hit upon the following device. He took one of those metallic blanches we have spoken of in the section on whitening the skin, moistened it to a half liquid, and tinged it with fine rouge to the exact color of the skin. This he spread in a thin film, véry exactly and evenly over the tattoo marks, and then taking an instrument formed of several fine needles, pricked the skin, so as to allow the paste to enter, and form a layer above the carbon. This answered the purpose completely, and the last emblem of the republic disappeared from Sweden. As we have said, this process can be repeated with uniform success, and it is the only process which holds out any prospect of concealing such marks. It can also be extended to certain varieties of birth-marks, discolored scars, and stains from explosions of gunpowder. Occasionally it may wear, and require to be repeated after some years, but this is no serious matter.

REDNESS OF THE SKIN.

Poor Bardolph suffered many a fling from fat Falstaff for his red face and fiery nose, which Sir John averred had saved him a thousand marks in links and torches, walking in the night twixt tavern and tavern. Not many, who are afflicted with this permanent and mortifying redness of the skin, can bear it as philosophically as Bardolph did, though they have it from a far more innocent cause.

Some persons suffer with it particularly in the nose, a situation that gives rise to unpleasant suspicions.

"Where could I have gotten this nose?" exclaimed Madame d'Albret once, in the presence of Matta, a wit of the Court of Louis XIV., a tendency to flushing being visible in that feature.

"At the sideboard, madam," was the prompt suggestion of the wit.

Not only the face, but the hands too, are liable to become suffused with a lasting flush, and not from any inclination to sack and sugar either, though an uncharitable world is ever ready to lend an ear to such a whisper.

Sometimes, as we have remarked, it comes from long exposure to heat, as in cooks, and those much in the sun. More frequently it is a debility of the minute vessels in the skin. Their coats become relaxed, and allow the blood to accumulate in their meshes. The treatment is therefore twofold. The debility must be

removed by gentle friction, cold bathing, tonics of iron
and bark, ergotin, and similar drugs, while the vessels
are stimulated by astringent washes, such as the following:—

Take—

Tannic acid	fifteen grains ;
Camphor water	five ounces.

Dissolve, and use several times a day, letting it dry on
the surface.

Simple spirits of camphor is another suitable lotion
when the redness is not decided. But when it is gone
to the extent that on closely examining the skin fine
red veins are perceptible, traversing it in various directions, then the case demands more active remedies,
which can only be properly administered by a physician.

ARSENIC-EATING, AND SECRET WASHES.

Within a few months we have noted three deaths at-
tributed by the newspapers to eating arsenic in order
to improve the complexion. The fact that such a custom has been widely prevalent for years is no secret to
most physicians. There is a preparation largely sold
by the shops under the attractive name *poudre rajeu-
nissante*, the active principle of which is simply arsenic,
or "ratsbane," as the old folks call it. The custom
has been immemorial in the Austrian Alps. The
peasants commence taking a small portion of *hidri*, as
they term it, an arsenical compound, four or five times

a week, when they are about eighteen or twenty years of age, and continue the habit, gradually increasing the quantity but not the frequency of the dose, as long as they live. Elderly people take as much as four grains at a time.

It does not seem to shorten their lives, or undermine their strength. On the contrary, they are, as we can say from personal observation, a handsome, sturdy, long-winded, and long-lived set. But the habit once commenced, it is said that it cannot with safety be discontinued, as either symptoms of poisoning or else some fatal disease soon carries the victim off.

The value of this potent drug in treating diseases and discolorations of the skin cannot be over-estimated. But the propriety of using it constantly for its cosmetic effects is, in spite of the example just quoted, open to very grave objections.

In the first place, there are constitutions on which it has, even in the minutest doses, a violently irritating effect. Again, if once commenced it may become unsafe to discontinue it, and who would wish to be tied down to this unnatural diet all their lives? There are other reasons not less weighty. Within the last score of years, since wall-papers colored with arsenical dyes (especially green paper) have come into vogue, physicians have been obliged to treat a number of persons poisoned by the minute amounts of arsenic floating in the atmosphere of rooms thus papered. Such being the case, it is altogether likely that a woman who is an arsenic-eater exhales from her person a sufficient amount of the poison to render her most undesirable for a wife, unless she occupies a separate apartment. Otherwise, she may share the fate of the damsel Sara, mentioned in the Apocrypha, the heroine of the book of Tobit, who had had seven husbands, all of whom were destroyed on the marriage night by an evil spirit. For the emanations from her body will certainly carry with them minute particles of the poisonous metal. The only reason that this is not the fate of the Styrian and Tyrolese damsels is, that with them lover and lady are both accustomed to use the drug. Like Mithridates, they have by long habit rendered themselves poison-proof.

It is somewhat singular that the drugs which at present are most in renown as cosmetics for the skin, are precisely the most deadly poisons known in the whole catalogue of chemical products. They are arsenic, prussic acid, corrosive sublimate, and caustic potash. As there are always dealers unscrupulous enough to sacrifice their own consciences (if they keep the article) and their customers' lives by selling, under sounding names, these perilous stuffs, we urgently warn all persons to be exceedingly cautious in making such purchases.

ERUPTIONS OF THE SKIN.

Most skin diseases are characterized, and indeed classified in books, by an eruption or breaking-out on the surface. These affections are so numerous, and often so difficult to distinguish apart, that it is out of the question for us to do more than glance at some which are common, and readily recognized. It would seem as if nature had designed to dash the pride of beauty by imposing on the skin of woman a greater liability to such defects. Or if you wish a less recondite cause, it is because, as a rule, she has a thinner, finer, and more sensitive skin.

She is unusually subject to such disorders at what are called in scientific language her "climacteric periods," that is, at puberty, during pregnancy, and at the change of life. Diseases peculiar to her sex lead to them with almost inevitable certainty, and the physician must first acquaint himself with her most intimate history, ere he can intelligently prepare to combat these blots on the scutcheon of beauty. Often, too, he will with the Roman general Fabius,

> "Qui cunctando restituit rem,"

counsel delay as the best part of valor and the wisest act of practice. Not that he will be much afraid of "driving in" one of these eruptions. This terror belongs to an obsolete epoch of medical science. Except at the periods we have just referred to, we cannot cure too quickly any skin disease. But at those times, especially during pregnancy, we must look cautiously to the effects of our medicines on the rest of the system, and on a being yet unborn. When nature is putting forth all her power to accomplish one of these mysterious transformations, or is engaged in the sublime and primal act of creation, the man is foolhardy who "without great argument" will interfere in her subtle processes.

These eruptions are either dry, covering the skin with thousands of minute scales like bran, or contain some fluid or half-fluid substance which oozes or can be pressed from them. Many of them are accompanied with discolorations of the skin, and with more or less pain. The pain, however, is in many of them less annoying than the *itching*. This is at times almost insupportable, and it may be present where there is no eruption visible whatever. Old people frequently are disturbed at night by it, and some girls and women, in perfect health apparently, are most seriously distressed by intolerable itching in divers parts. We know the case of a married lady, who during each pregnancy was almost driven wild by this distress. The family physician exhausted all his resources without doing the least good. One day when a toothache was added to her other miseries, her husband told her to take a few whiffs of his cigar in order to soothe the tooth. She did so, and as if by magic the itching entirely left her.

She found by smoking for a few minutes several times a day she could live with perfect comfort. It is not likely that the remedy would have so desirable an effect on every one, as the complaint is extremely obstinate.

The itching and burning with which girls are affected often depend upon worms, or upon some disturbance of the digestion.

The parts can be washed several times a day with one of these lotions, which should not be wiped off:—

> Take—
>
> Powdered borax   a half ounce ;
> Rain water   a pint.
>
> **Mix.**

Or,

Take hyposulphite of soda, and water, the same quantities.

Or this unguent:—

> Take—
>
> Bicarbonate of soda   two ounces :
> Tincture of benzoin   one ounce.

Mix, and rub a small portion on the part while in bed.

As we have said, there may be no eruption whatever, and yet the severest itching. Therefore, except as the skin is torn by scratching, such complaints hardly come within our present scheme. But when some visible sign is present, especially on the exposed parts, it is time for active interference. The women of to-day must not despair, like Anne of Austria, wife of Louis XIII., of France.

That noble dame suffered from an eruption on her body which could not be cured. At length it invaded her hands and face. When she thus found herself disfigured, she took to her bed, and saying: "It is time for me to depart," refused all attentions, and died. However severe such eruptions may be, very few are beyond the reach of modern medical science.

PIMPLES, HIVES, CARBUNCLES, ETC.

On every square inch of the skin there are hundreds and hundreds of little openings, through which the perspiration finds an exit, or in which the hairs are planted. These openings lead to short canals which descend into the true skin. Besides the perspiration, the sides of these canals secrete a fatty substance which gives to the skin its oiliness and smoothness.

Sometimes the aperture of one of the canals becomes choked, and the fatty secretion, instead of flowing out, is penned in and hardens. The portion of it at the aperture becomes dirty and black, and forms one of those small black specks on the face, which common people call "grubs," from the belief that they are the black heads of little worms. They can be readily pressed out after washing the face with soap, and anointing it with glycerine.

When for some reason the health is not robust, as for instance when young people are growing too rapidly, a canal or sweat-gland which is thus stopped up may become inflamed, red, and swollen, forming a *pimple*, or what the French call *couperose*. Pimples are the despair of beauty, and many a young girl is annoyed by them beyond all expression. We have all seen not a few faces spoiled by them, and not only are they most apt to occur at that period of life when we are most solicitous about our personal appearance, but in the large majority of cases the female sex are the sufferers.

Indiscretions in diet may cause them, and it is said that coffee especially predisposes to them, as it may also to a darkening of the skin.

They are very frequent again about the change of life, and some women have them whenever they are with child. They usually are associated with some alteration in the general health, and, as a rule, are very obstinate, disfiguring the complexion for years unless properly treated.

As they so often depend upon some constitutional irregularity, which must first be remedied, and which can only be done by a physician, the cures we are about to suggest, though often successful, are not always so. They may be tried, and if they do not succeed, it may be taken as a hint that the case is beyond domestic medication.

A very useful wash is the borax and glycerine lotion which we gave on a previous page. It should be used several times a day, and allowed to remain on the face.

A teaspoonful of powdered alum dissolved in a tumbler of water is another often successful wash, which should be applied in the same manner.

If, after trying either of these for a fortnight, no benefit is apparent, then the face should be washed with strong soft soap at night, and the pimples smeared with a paste made of flowers of sulphur and spirits of camphor. This should be washed off next morning, and the spots rubbed with a small quantity of glycerine.

Sea-bathing, or a visit to the Sulphur Springs of Virginia (either the White or the Red Sulphur), or those equally efficient sulphurous sources in Florida, or washing with sulphur soap, will be of great avail. A bath of some kind should be taken daily, and the skin well rubbed, as by this means the pores of the whole body are opened, and those of the face have therefore less to do.

Such pimples are most common on the forehead and cheeks. There is another variety still more annoying. They commence on the nose, and spread from it as a centre over the face. The surface is red, and swollen into small lumps, which the vulgar call "carbuncles," or "rum-blossoms," because the popular belief is that they generally come from hard-drinking. This is not true, for they are less frequent in men than in women. The suspicion they create is, however, very unpleasant, as well as the loss of beauty, and they are quite as common in the best classes of society as among the poor and needy. Francis the First, King of France, the same of whom it is related that he stooped to pick up the pencil of Titian, was afflicted with them for several years. He was even philosophical enough not to resent a joke at their expense. One day, in his wars with the Emperor Charles V., of Germany, he was expressing some anxiety about the safe-keeping of the crown-jewels. His brother, who stood by, dared to say:—

" Your majesty need give yourself no uneasiness about them. You always carry them under your own eyes."

The pun is broader in French, in which language these red swellings are familiarly called *rubis*, rubies.

The disease is often foreshadowed by flushing of the face and nose at meals, and whenever hot or spirituous drinks are taken. Though obstinate, it is curable, and so far from requiring a meagre diet, as so many people suppose, and consequently deny themselves even necessary food, it is a disease of debility, demanding plenty of good nourishing aliment. When quite recent, spirits of camphor which has been poured over fresh sliced horseradish is an efficient wash.

It is too often associated with some disorder of digestion, or with general feebleness, for local remedies only to avail much, so that we can but admonish those who suffer from it, or who are threatened with it, to put themselves on proper constitutional treatment.

Hives, or the *nettle-rash*, is a curious complaint from which some persons suffer very frequently. The skin becomes red, and swells in ridges, similar to those caused by the stings of a nettle, or a smart blow of a cowskin. We have seen instances where it appeared regularly after eating lobster, and in another case from an oyster supper.

There are any number of domestic remedies vaunted for it, not one of which is of much value. Too often it is constitutional, or else dependent upon some disorder of the digestive organs, for any simple application to do good. Washing with the borax and glycerine lotion promises well. Persons who are subject to it should not wear flannel next the skin, should be very careful about their diet, and should use some stimulating lotion (a pint of camphor water with one teaspoonful of tincture of red pepper) once or twice a week.

Heat rash, or *prickly heat*, is an invariable concomitant of hot weather, with some whose skins are delicate. Children suffer much from it. A cooling lotion, such as a few teaspoonfuls of dilute solution of the subacetate of lead in a half pint of water, or a heaping spoonful of baking soda in the same quantity, or a mixture of vinegar and water, will often relieve the heat and burning.

One cannot examine too suspiciously any eruption or spot on the face. Sometimes the neglect of an apparently insignificant pimple has resulted most sadly.

There is a terrible disease called significantly *lupus*, the wolf, on account of the fearful ravages it causes when once established. Not another complaint in the long and dismal catalogue of maladies leads to such horrible deformity, gnawing, as it does, flesh, bone, bloodvessels, one after another, quite away. We speak of it with the greater emphasis because its victims are most commonly young, robust looking, previously healthy women, and because at its outset it masks itself under such an insignificant form, that it is apt to be overlooked.

"Such is the deceptive mode of its approach," says the English surgeon, Mr. Thomas Hunt, "that the physician is almost as liable as the patient to mistake it at first for some trifling disease." It commences nearly always with a small tender pimple or sore spot on, close by, or within the nose. Whenever such a one is noticed, it is of the utmost importance to institute a close examination, "for," says the same writer, "if it should prove to be lupus, a brief delay will be sure to produce more or less deformity, and the beauty of the patient will be irrecoverably lost." Its treatment must be early and decisive. Too much care cannot be taken to prevent it fastening on the tissues. All scabs, sores, and pimples in this region should therefore be regarded suspiciously, and if they seem slow in healing, a surgeon's advice should be sought.

From this distressing foe of beauty we shall pass to some by no means so appalling, but nevertheless quite worthy our attention. Some faces are sown with minute, hard, white pimples in the skin, from the size of a pin's head to that of a pea. They are painless, but ruin the beauty of the complexion, and should, therefore, be removed. They occur at all periods of life, and as fate decrees that there shall be many reminders to humble the pride of comeliness, so they are most frequent in the young. The eyelid, both on the inner and the outer side, is one of their chosen seats.

Those who are subject to them should wash daily with soap containing tar, such as can now be readily obtained from druggists. As for removing them, there is only one way known, and that is by puncturing them with the point of an extremely sharp lancet, and squeezing out the contents. No scar will be left if the little operation is carefully done.

We have already spoken of warts on the hands. They are bad enough in that position, but what shall we say to them on the face? Almost daily, in walking through the streets of this city, we see handsome faces and necks marred by these ugly excrescences. Why they are allowed to remain is a constant puzzle to us, when they can be surely and promptly removed, leaving no scar, or at worst a small bleached spot. and this with little and often no pain. We have already referred to some of the means employed to destroy them, and may here add that where they are numerous and apt to recur, as is the case with some persons, a course of internal treatment under medical advice should be commenced which will effectually dispel any such tendency. Warty faces convey an impression of vulgarity, because one associates them with neglect of personal care, and a coarse diet.

There are many other varieties of tumors in the skin and immediately beneath it. Some of these, such as wens, which are so common on the heads of many persons, can only be remedied by the surgeon's knife. Others, especially such as are found on the neck, under the chin, and in front of the ears, are what are called glandular, and not hastily to be meddled with in this manner. Against them, galvanism and electricity are our weapons, and often we are able to disperse them or reduce them very considerably by these powerful agents, without the use of any other means whatever. We shall not go into a discussion of the apparatus employed, and the method found most successful to accomplish this, for the professional man can find it elsewhere, and the readers whom we address will not design to apply it on themselves. Suffice it if we assure them that until this means has been fully tried, they should not rest content to carry about such a deformity.

THE PREVENTION AND REMOVAL OF SCARS.

Whenever the face or the hands are cut, burned, or otherwise injured, it is of the utmost importance to see that the least possible scar is left. The parts should be carefully washed with cold water, until they are thoroughly cleaned and no longer bleed, and then the edges brought together very exactly, and fastened with sticking plaster. In large wounds, the care of a surgeon will be necessary to prevent deformity. Burns are peculiarly liable to leave behind them ugly marks, which it is next to impossible to diminish. We must, therefore, aim to conceal them, which, in some instances, can be very satisfactorily done by the method of tattooing with flesh-colored tints, to which we have alluded previously.

What is worse than this about these scars from burns and scalds is the tendency they have to contract, pulling the features and neighboring parts into the most frightfully deformed positions. During the process of healing, the surgeon will overcome this in great measure by elastic straps and proper apparatus. When it has once taken place, the cure is difficult. Still, for the term of a year after the injury, the scar is still pliable enough to be stretched. When it refuses these gentle means, it must be attacked with the surgeon's knife. It is true that it is often one of the most delicate and difficult operations in surgery to remedy these contractions, but with great patience among all concerned, it can generally be successfully carried through, and the parts, though never equal to what they might have been, will no longer be frightful or disgusting in appearance. Thus, an eyelid permanently drawn down, a chin fastened to the neck, two fingers grown together, or an ear pulled out of position, may be very much amended.

Thanks to Lady Mary Wortley Montague, who introduced inoculation from Turkey, and to Dr. Jenner, who discovered vaccination, it is a rare sight now-a-days to see any one in the higher walks of life pitted by the smallpox. In former times, it used to be the terror of life to every one who had a pretty face, for there was no means known to prevent it leaving its hideous traces, even if life itself was not lost. Now, we can but rarely entirely do away with, or conceal the pits it digs, but very much may be done to prevent the attack, and in those rare instances where that fails to protect the individuals the scarring can be almost wholly avoided by timely local applications. So that not only in a medical but in a cosmetic point of view, our century has here won a manifest victory.

Even those faces which are pitted by the disease can

22

always be improved, and some very considerably so. For this purpose, strong stimulating lotions are employed several times daily, alternated with gentle and long-continued inunction of oil or glycerine. In many instances, by steady perseverance in such applications very great improvement has resulted.

ON WRINKLES.

What cosmetic artist would not give one of his fingers to know some simple, efficacious means to do away with the furrows which Time leaves in the brow and cheeks? It has occupied the thoughts of many a one, and we could tell of dozens of processes suggested. They are different in plan, but in one respect are all alike, and that is, they are all of no avail.

The only suggestions we have to make are preventive, not curative. Let the skin be maintained in a soft, pliable, healthy condition, avoid frowning and grimaces which contract the muscles of the face, do not sit by a bright light which forces you to squint and half close the eyes, and maintain as much command as possible over the facial muscles.

It has been supposed that when once the skin has been thus corrugated into folds, it were possible, by stretching it with adhesive strips, to restore it to its natural evenness and smoothness. This has failed in every instance we have known it tried, and we consider it time thrown away. Undoubtedly half the lines which seam the face of maturity are not those of years, but of passion, of chagrin, or of habitual contortion of the muscles. They can therefore be prevented, and when they are just beginning to show themselves, they can be diminished by a strong exertion of self-command.

In the artificial courts of the last century, and in certain circles of our day, it was and is the custom to plaster these inequalities with a sort of "enamel," a ridiculous and harmful usage, which can only be done at the expense of an injury to the skin, and, what is not less pardonable, it can inevitably be detected by an eye at all practised in cosmetic arts.

THE HAIR.

IF we were inclined to commence this chapter with a text, we should have no difficulty in finding an appropriate one. For example, these words of St. Paul:—

"If a woman have long hair, it is a glory to her."

Or if our wish is to choose a graceful motto from some poet, what neater lines could be found than these:—

> "Fair tresses man's imperial race ensnare,
> And beauty draws us with a single hair."

All writers, sacred and profane, ancient and modern, join in praising with unstinted terms the advantages which personal comeliness derives from a handsome head of hair.

In all ages women have been deeply sensitive of it, and even when fashion decreed that the flowing locks should be cropped, it was only to supply their place with artificial ones of more luxuriant amplitude. Few willingly forego the advantages it gives. The Duchess of Marlborough, wife of the "great Duke," was a termagant of the worst sort. No anecdote so forcibly illustrates her temper as this: She had long and rich hair, which her husband greatly admired. One day, to spite him, she cropped it off close and threw it in his face.

But she was of a nature to defy death itself. When very old, she was taken sick. The physicians told her she must be blistered. She refused. They urged it. She remained obstinate. At length one of them said, "Unless your ladyship is willing to be blistered you will die." "I won't be blistered and I won't die," returned the incorrigible old woman. And for that time she was as good as her word.

Her daughter inherited her disposition, and between them both the Duke, who was an affectionate husband and father, had a trying time. He dryly remarked to his daughter one day:—

"I wonder you and your mother do not agree better. You are so much alike."

But a truce to these stories. We set out to write a chapter on the hair, and not the History of England. We shall begin at once with a few words on the

PHYSIOLOGY OF THE HAIR.

When a hair is pulled from the head, we observe that the end which was implanted in the scalp is larger than the shaft. This portion is the bulb or root of the hair. It is firmly fixed in the true skin or derma, and from it, as the tree from its root, the hair draws its sustenance. The shaft, when examined by a microscope, is seen in straight hairs to be nearly or quite round, but more or less flattened when the hair is wavy or curly, for the flattening of the hair causes this curliness.

If a hair is drawn between the fingers from its root to its point, it feels smooth, but when drawn from its point to its root, it leaves a sensation of roughness. This is because each hair is covered with minute scales, in appearance like those on a fish or a snake, disposed from root to point, one overlapping the other like slates on a steeple.

Beneath this layer of scales is a mass of fibrous cells, in shape like spindles, which form the body of the hair. They contain the coloring matter which imparts to the hair its hue. Through the centre of the hair, from root to tip, is a very minute canal filled with air. So that in fact a hair is a delicate tube with two walls, the inner one of strong fibrous cells containing coloring matter, the outer one of flat scales.

Everybody knows what a difference there is in the size of hairs. Some are fine and silky, others coarse and bristly. But every one does not know that the coarsest hair is found in women. We would naturally suppose that men would have it, but it is not so. The finest hair occurs in children, especially those who are scrofulous. The difference is considerable. The diameter of some hairs is twelve or thirteen times greater than that of others.

It is a vain task, one might suppose, to set to work to number the hairs of the head. "As the hairs of the head, or the sands of the sea in number," is a favorite Oriental metaphor to express an innumerable host. Yet there are those who have attempted this incredible labor. Nor is it a very great task to make some approximation. Thus we know there are one hundred and twenty square inches covered with hair, on a head of average size. Take a single square inch, where the hairs seem of an average thickness, and count how many there are. It can be done in a short time. The result will be, in a healthy scalp, from eight hundred to twelve hundred, say in round numbers one thousand. Multiply this by one hundred and twenty, and we have one hundred and twenty thousand as the average number of hairs on the head.

In the early ages the Frankish kings used to pluck a single hair and bestow it on one of their attendants as a (cheap and) significant token of their favor. Few of them but might have so rewarded every one of their subjects without materially thinning the covering which nature had given their heads.

The fine short hairs over the body are not nearly so thick. For instance, since writing the last paragraph, we have marked out on our forearm the area of one square inch, and carefully counted the hairs it contains. There are eighty-five in all, and this is more than authors say are usually found.

The growth of the hair in a healthy scalp is from eight to ten inches a year. Its rapidity is not the same at all times. A German writer who has given great attention to this small matter (if, indeed, any of the operations of nature should be called small) has found that it grows faster in the daytime than at night, and in the summer than the winter. There is a common notion that the increase is also more marked in the first half of the lunar month, and there are not wanting men of science who have indorsed this belief. "Who does not know by his own experience," confidently says the Abbe Toaldo in his *Saggio Meteorologico*, "that the hair and nails grow faster after the new, than after the full moon?" To which question most physicians coolly reply that nobody knows it. As it is a matter of one's own experience, we recommend every one who is curious about it to observe for himself, and make up his own mind irrespective of the agreement of doctors.

Many persons are alarmed toward the close of summer and the commencement of autumn, to discover their hair coming out in unusual quantity. There is commonly no ground for anxiety. This is a natural and healthy occurrence, similar to the moulting of fowls, or the change of coat in deer, cats, and other hairy animals. The hairs reach their maturity, die, fall out, and are replaced by others, but to a less extent in man than in those animals.

Children who are born with hair lose it all in a few months, though the change is hardly noticed, as the new hair is substituted so gradually. During a fever or a sea voyage, it is not unusual for the hair to fall out, but it is very rare for the baldness to remain, if proper precautions are observed. So long as the hair-bulbs are healthy, the hair can be made to grow; when they are destroyed or absorbed, then the baldness is irremediable, and it is useless and foolish to attempt any course of treatment to restore it. If the skin has a white, shiny, polished appearance, if it does not easily become red when rubbed, if on examining it with a microscope, a number of small hairs are not visible, and the ducts of the hair-bulbs are closed, then the patient had better spend no more money on " hair restorers," " philocomes," or " trichogenes," but save it for his *perruquier.*

The color of the hair we have explained to be dependent on the coloring matter in the cells of the inner coat. It varies in health from a light flaxen to a jet black, and can to some extent be altered by the materials taken as food, and also by applications made directly to the external surface of the scalp.

THE HAIR IN HEALTH—WASHING, COMBING, AND BRUSHING.

The skin of the scalp, like that of any other part of the body, must be kept clean in order to be healthy. We do not, however, recommend it to be washed too often. It is no small labor for a woman with long and thick tresses to give her head a thorough ablution. Once a week is as often as we can ask her to do it.

The materials needed are a fine sponge, soft, tepid water, and a mild neutral soap, white Castile being as good as any. The locks should be parted, and the sponge, moistened, but not dripping, should be rubbed on the scalp, not on the hair. The hair needs no washing, but only the skin. After the head has been cleansed, the soap should be carefully removed by the sponge and pure water, and the hair dried with a soft towel.

Instead of the soap and water, many prefer the yelk of an egg beaten up in a tumbler of warm water, and it makes an excellent application. There are also circumstances, as, for instance, where soft water is not convenient, when a hair-wash may be used to advantage. We shall suggest several of these, which can be readily prepared, and which are suitable for frequent use on healthy heads.

Dissolve half an ounce of transparent soap in a quart of rain water. Add a small wineglassful of alcohol, and a few drops of some aromatic oil. Let it stand a few days before using, shaking it occasionally.

Or this :—

Borax in powder	a teaspoonful ;
Soft water	a quart ;
Oil of lavender	sufficient to scent.

Or this :—

Aromatic spirits of ammonia,
Best olive oil, of each a tablespoonful.

Mix them well together, then add slowly a pint of rain water, and scent with rondeletia, or otto of roses, or whatever aroma is preferred.

After the scalp has been thus thoroughly cleansed, it is unnecessary to use any oil or pomatum whatever, as the natural secretion of the skin is sufficient. If, however, either of the above washes seems to leave the hair dry and the skin harsh, a few teaspoonfuls of pure glycerine may be added to the receipt.

It is of great importance in washing the head, as well as in brushing or dressing it, not to pull or jerk the hair. Everything must be done gently, as violence breaks, splits, and loosens the hairs, ultimately causing them to fall out and leave bare spots.

There is a precept in hair-dressing which cannot be too widely known. It is this :—

Wash the scalp, but not the hair ; comb the hair, but not the scalp.

Except in diseased conditions of the skin, there is no occasion for scratching it with a sharp-pointed comb, or a hard brush. Such irritation frequently leads to disease, and should be avoided. Combs are for arranging and cleansing the hair. They should be of several sizes, their teeth blunt, and entirely free from cracks, splinters, or broken points. If a single tooth is broken or split, the comb should be discarded. Buffalo horn, tortoise shell, ivory, vulcanized rubber, are all unobjectionable materials, though the latter is often inconvenient on account of the electricity it develops.

A coarse comb should first be used to loosen the hair from knots, and then a fine comb to cleanse it from dust or powder.

Several brushes are required to dress the hair properly. One should be soft and yielding, with which the scalp itself should be brushed. Another of firmer bristles is requisite to brush out the hair, and clean it more thoroughly than the comb. And a third should be devoted to applying any oil or similar application, which may be used. For this latter purpose, the ingenuity of perfumers has devised a special form of brush, with a hollow back in which the oil or lotion is poured, and by which it can be applied without greasing the hands or dripping on the clothing.

As the hairs have a natural direction in coming through the skin, it is well to brush and comb them always in this direction, and never against it, and still less to rub them from the tip toward the root. Any such proceeding weakens them. When the mode prescribes the hair to be dressed contrary to its usual growth, as in the *frisure à la Chinoise*, and *à l'Empresse Eugénie*, this direction must be given them gently, and without unnecessary combing.

After the scalp is washed, the hair should be put up loosely for several hours, and avoidance of exposure to the sun or out-door air for the same length of time is altogether advisable.

Whenever a person with long hair expects to be sick for any length of time, the hair should be firmly plaited, but without straining the roots, and not disturbed so long as it feels comfortable. During and after a fever it is very apt to fall, but will be quite sure to grow again, especially if it is kept closely cut, and some stimulant application, such as we shall describe hereafter, is regularly employed.

This leads us to consider the general question of

CUTTING THE HAIR.

It is curious how people, even professional specialists in the treatment of the hair, differ on the propriety and results of clipping it. Some maintain that it is one of the most important points in its preservation, while others declare it is of no use whatever, or positively injurious. For instance, we have in our hands a book on skin diseases by Dr. Tilbury Fox, a very high

23

authority among our English cousins. He says, "Shaving the scalp is beneficial. Nine out of ten affirm that this does harm. I know to the contrary."

We have a friend, a surgeon in the navy, who is one of the nine. He was on duty in the East India squadron, and for some cause, he could not imagine what, his hair commenced falling out. He thereupon shaved his head, and what was his annoyance to find that the hairs never would grow again! You may be sure he does not indorse Dr. Tilbury Fox.

Men keep their hair closely cropped, and have done so as a rule ever since history commenced. Yet it is matter of daily observation that their hair is weaker than woman's, more apt to fall out, and more subject to disease. This has been explained by all sorts of theories. Some have blamed "stove-pipe hats," some the custom of more completely covering the head and thus shutting out the air. others attribute it to the greater activity of the brain in man (absurd people!), others claim the difference is owing to the greater pains women take with their hair, and others accuse cutting the locks as the cause of their downfall. But it is likely that all are wrong, and that it is one of the physiological peculiarities of the male sex. to have weaker. as we have already stated that it is to have finer hair (that is. of less diameter). The apostle Paul. who. though no physiologist by profession, was a man of consummate ability, and educated in all the wisdom of both Jews and Greeks, was clearly of this opinion when he said (1 Corinthians xi. 14):—

"Doth not even nature itself teach you that if a man have long hair it is a shame unto him?" Meaning, evidently, that nature had reserved for the other sex superior strength and durability of the hair.

If this is so, then the argument against cutting does not find support here. Moreover, a wide and carefully noted experience shows that the hair is strengthened, and its growth is more rapid, if frequently clipped. One of those pains-taking Germans. whose patience is only equalled by their accuracy, tells us that if a man shaves every twelve hours, his beard will grow from six to twelve inches a year, but if he shaves only once in thirty-six hours, it will grow but from four to six inches in the same time. This is true in principle for the hair elsewhere.

We shall commence our precepts with childhood. It is known that there is a feeble circulation in a hair. It is not dead, but living, and constantly draws nourishment from the fluids with which its root is surrounded. The longer it is, the more it demands from its root. Therefore, in children, while it is well always to give the root enough to do, it is not well to overwork it. Their hair should be kept at a medium length, say from three to six inches, by monthly clippings, until they are fourteen or fifteen years of age. Then it may be allowed to grow.

In older persons the plan that should be adopted is different. Their hair should be examined, scissors in hand, once a month, but not with a view of curtailing its length. The plan suggested by that distinguished writer on Skin Diseases, Mr. Erasmus Wilson, though a tedious one, is undoubtedly superior to all others. The locks, he recommends, should be carefully scrutinized, and wherever a hair is found with a split, a twisted, a dead, or a discolored extremity, it should be cut off down to the healthy portion. All others should be left undisturbed. By this simple procedure, the hair is sure to be maintained in full vigor, and will constantly increase in length. It may be somewhat tedious, but what woman who sets much store by her flowing locks would not be willing to devote say two or three hours a month to this procedure? We positively state that this is the only kind of hair-cutting which one with healthy hair should submit to under ordinary circumstances.

We make this latter proviso, for we have met cases where the hair had to be kept short for considerations of general health. Some women suffer much from headache, which will not yield to any treatment until the hair is shortened. Others have found that by some sympathy difficult to explain, the eyesight was improved by trimming their locks. Such instances are rare, but as they are so often overlooked, it is well to give them a passing mention. The sympathy between the hair and the eyes is said to be especially observable in children of a scrofulous constitution, and for that reason their hair should not be allowed to grow long.

HOW TO CURL AND STIFFEN THE HAIR.

Dishevelled locks are rarely in fashion. Much more frequently the decrees of the mode prescribe some frisure into which the rebellious tresses have to be forced against their will. To constrain them, certain preparations have been devised, known as *bandolines*, or *fixateurs* (the technical terms of the toilet are always derived from the French). We shall give several of them which are harmless, and may therefore be used without scruple. The simplest is soap and water, or water alone. But these are not always efficient. Here is a venerable and familiar one :—

Take—

Bruised quince seeds	a tablespoonful ;
Clean rain water	a pint.

Boil gently to three-quarters of a pint, then strain through muslin and add

Alcohol or brandy,
Cologne water,   of each two tablespoonfuls.

It can be applied by moistening the fingers and passing them through the hair, or, what is neater, by using for the purpose a small sponge.

The following is equally well adapted and easily compounded :—

Dissolve three ounces of clean powdered gum-arabic in half a pint of rose-water. Strain and add sufficient aniline red (about one drop of the solution) to give it a rosy color. This not only fixes. the hair in place, but lends it a peculiar brilliant gloss, very attractive. It is similar to the celebrated *Crême de mauve*, which is after all nothing but glycerine scented with extract of jessamine, and colored with aniline red. The striking tint which it gives the hair rendered it quite popular at once.

A small quantity of powdered alum is sometimes added to either of the above receipts, in order to render them still stronger, but usually they will be found to answer perfectly without this ingredient.

For the same purpose, hairdressers frequently employ what are called hard or stick pomatum (*bâtons fixateurs*). They are of wax with more or less animal fat, and scented and colored in various manners. Usually they are not injurious, but they leave a greasy appearance, and are inferior to the bandolines above mentioned.

Ladies need not be informed that to curl the hair, curling sticks and curl papers are the usual methods. The latter should not be wound too tight, as the strain upon the roots of the hair is hurtful to its growth. By judiciously using the mucilaginous washes just described, the hair will remain in curl or in waves without such violence being required.

Sometimes fashion approves of a thousand little ripples of hair over the head. It is no trifling matter to obey her behests here, without sacrificing the safety of the locks. Some lay hold of the curling tongs, and certainly this instrument brings about speedy results. Experience teaches, however, that the heat of the iron destroys the life of the hair, the slow circulation which we have mentioned is checked, and after a few years, if not sooner, the head loses it covering.

In Paris, and we suspect in this country too, hair-dressers employ for the same purpose the powerful mixture used by the dealers in furs to curl and twist the hair on the skins they make into muffs, etc. This is a solution of quicksilver in nitric acid. Some of it is diluted with an equal amount of water; the hair is moistened with it for several inches from the head, care being taken not to let any of the fluid touch the scalp. The locks are then placed loosely in the crimps it is wished to give them, and rapidly dried by a stove or in a draft of warm air. After several hours they are thoroughly washed with warm water. The curl remains for several weeks or even longer. But the process is a deleterious one, as the acid eats into the hair and destroys its vitality. This is the preparation sold under the name of *sécretage*, or " permanent curling fluid." We do not give the formula, as we do not approve of its use, and no one who confines the arts of the toilet within the limits prescribed by the laws of health and good sense, will permit themselves to use it or have it applied.

HAIR-POWDERS.

Within a few years the ancient custom of powdering the hair has come again into vogue. In the last century it was almost universal, and one of William Pitt's famous methods of raising the revenue was to tax hair-powder. He estimated, in 1795, that the amount of flour annually consumed for this purpose in the United Kingdom represented the enormous and incredible value of six million dollars! This must have been excessive.

When we called it an ancient custom we may not have been correct, as it cannot be traced further back than the end of the sixteenth century. Singular to say, the first who introduced it were the nuns in the French convents. Those who had occasion to leave temporarily the walls of the cloisters for any purpose were wont to powder their hair, so as to make it appear gray, and give them a venerable and aged look. The fashionable dames were struck with the excellent and novel effect of white powder on dark hair, and soon appropriated the device as one of the arts of the worldly toilet. The reverend fathers probably thought that here was another instance where the livery of heaven had been seized to serve the devil in, and now-a-days we do not hear of any nuns who continue the usage.

For our part, we disagree with the reverend fathers (if they entertained the notion we have ascribed to them), the judicious use of innocuous powders being not in the least hurtful to the hair, and adding unquestionably, in some instances, to its beauty.

The powder usually employed is simply potato starch, ground very fine, passed through a gauze sieve, and scented. It is not, however, the most elegant. To obtain this, the fashionable world levies a contribution upon the icy North, in order to scatter over the heads of its favorites the simulated snows of age. The moss which the reindeer feeds on is dug from under the drifts, assorted and pulverized. It yields a fragrant, grayish-white powder, which is mingled with an equal part of finest starch, and sold under the name of " Cyprus powder." This is prized beyond any other in the boudoirs of Europe.

Whenever the hair is powdered, the following morning it should be carefully washed, and the scalp cleansed with soap and water. Attention should be given that none of the powder remains in or behind the ears, or on the skin, as the secretions of the body soon change it into an irritating mass. In placing it on the hair, if the latter is dry, a very small quantity of glycerine should be used to moisten it, and no more powder be added than will cling to the hairs, as it is exceedingly disagreeable to have it flying about at every motion or draught of air. None of it should be allowed to fall on the face, or enter the eyes.

In 1860, the Empress Eugenie set the fashion of using gold powder on some occasions. This has been followed to some extent in this country, but instead of gold powder, which is of course exorbitantly dear, bronze powder is used, which is very similar in appearance. Probably both of these metallic substances are hurtful to the hair, but as they would only be applied on rare occasions, we need not preach a philippic against them.

GRAY HAIR, AND HAIR-DYES.

Gray hair is not always a sign of years. Many persons have it long before the age of decrepitude, and some from earliest childhood. In more than one instance we have seen it in boys and girls, while it is not at all infrequent to find " a sable silvered" on heads over which not thirty winters have sprinkled their snows.

Much depends upon the original color of the hair. Black and dark brown change sooner than light brown, red, or flaxen, and of course in the former the contrast is more marked. There is a shade of light brown which seems almost never to turn gray. We have seen it preserving its natural hue to the age of fourscore and beyond.

One of those popular beliefs, long current among the people and long discredited by physicians, but at length conceded by all, is the influence which the mind exerts in changing the color and affecting the growth of the hair. Whether it be that the hair is planted so near the brain, or whether it be that it is so intimately dependent on the nervous system, we do not know, but certain it is that great anxieties, trouble, violent emotions, especially of a dismal character, discolor or debilitate the hair.

This is not extraordinary. Not the hair only, but every part of our system is preserved by serenity of mind, freedom from sorrow, avoidance of passion, absence of care, strong desire, or fear. It is not so much time as trouble that

> "Doth transfix the flourish set on youth,
> And delves the parallels in Beauty's brow."

Would you learn the composition of the real elixir of life? Seek it not in the volumes of medical or alchemical lore, but in serenity, cheerfulness, and content.

Fontenelle, who lived a hundred years, and was Secretary of the Academy of Sciences for more than half that period, owed his longevity to such a disposition. He even carried it to the extent of impassiveness. One day he spoke to Madame Tencin in a very calm manner about some occurrence, which he averred touched him to the heart.

"Heart!" exclaimed she, provoked at his apparent want of feeling, "heart! You have no heart. You are nothing but brains where your heart should be."

This disposition Fontenelle inherited from his mother. She was niece of the celebrated dramatist Corneille, a pious and excellent woman, but not easily moved. Fontenelle used to say of her: "My mother was a quietist. When I would express some unorthodox opinion before her, she would say, 'My son, you will be damned.' But it did not trouble her."

Gray hairs and wrinkles are slow in coming to such temperaments.

On the contrary, intense grief blanches the hair in a few hours. Every one is familiar with the opening lines of Byron's Prisoner of Chillon:—

> "My hair is gray but not with years,
> Nor turned it white
> In a single night,
> As men's have done with sudden fears."

In a note, the poet mentions Ludovico Sforza as the example he had in mind. The story is this: Ludovico Sforza, called from his dark complexion Ludovico the Moor, was Duke of Milan at the close of the fifteenth century. He was a cruel and unscrupulous man, as were all the Italian rulers of his day, from Alexander Sixth downward. By his political action, but especially by poisoning a nobleman who was under French protection, he drew upon himself the enmity of

France, was attacked, defeated, and driven from his dominions.

He collected another army of Swiss and Italians, and encountered the foreign hosts once more on the battle-field. The conflict would have been decided in his favor, but the Swiss had been secretly bribed by the French, and in the heat of action withdrew. The Italians were panic-stricken and fled. Ludovico, deserted by all but one or two attendants, took the clothes from the dead body of a peasant, and sought to escape in this disguise. He almost accomplished his purpose, but at nightfall was recognized by a cavalryman, seized, and dragged to prison. Alone in the gloomy cell, the duke pondered the livelong, sleepless night on the past, with its glorious and misused opportunities, and on the blank and hopeless future. The next morning the gaoler found in the cell a wan and gray-haired man, instead of the raven-locked and handsome nobleman he had shut in the night before. In one night, grief and fear had done the work of years. His terrors were not without foundation, for those chains never left his limbs till they were struck off his corpse.

Such instances are by no means rare, and we could readily name many other characters distinguished in history, whose sufferings, proportionate to their powers and prospects, have prematurely, and in a very short time, blanched their locks.

24

It is of more interest, however, to inquire into the general causes which are at work in bringing about this unwelcome change. The fact is familiar that in the large majority of cases we find, on examining a head about becoming gray, that single hairs are gray throughout their whole length, while others retain their original color. We do not find a hair black at the extremity and white at the root, as we might expect, nor do we find others passing through the intermediate hues between gray, and that natural to the person. What we do find is a single, long, silvery thread, winding conspicuous and ominous among the raven tresses.

This is because when a hair turns gray it loses its pigment promptly—in a few hours or a few days throughout its whole length—owing to absorption by the root, or some chemical or mechanical change in the hair itself.

There are some persons who turn gray very early without visible cause, and in some families premature grayness is hereditary. Sometimes a single lock of the hair, or one spot on the head, alters in color, while all the remainder is unchanged. To explain such vagaries is not easy.

Very respectable authorities say that when gray hair falls out, it does not grow again. This may be the rule, but we have known exceptions to it. A lady of our acquaintance lost all her hair, which was gray,

during an illness. After her recovery a new growth
appeared, thick and curly, but of the same silvery hue.

Whatever the cause, extent, or manner of the grayness may be, the practical question is, how to conceal
it, if concealment is desired. There are some faces
which appear more pleasing with silvery locks, and at
a certain age (we will not venture to give figures) it is
uncomely to simulate the tresses of youth, when the
ravages of years are too plainly visible on the features
and the form. In premature grayness no good reason
can be offered against hiding the disfigurement.

Can the natural color be restored by diet or by
drugs? Many writers and many charlatans aver that
it can. The latter are ready to hand out some secret
fluid "which is not a dye," the former speak of food
rich in carbon and iron, tonic medicines, and such
other chemical elements as analysis reveals in dark
hair.

We believe that none of these means will with certainty arrest the tendency to grayness, and still less
will they bring the color to that which is already
blanched. The general experience is that grayness is
not a consequence of physical debility, or of an insuffi-
cient diet. Nor can any external application materially darken the hair, except as it acts either as a
paint or a dye. All claims to the contrary are of little
value, and when vehemently urged, cause us to suspect
the nostrum which puts them forth as unworthy of

confidence. We shall, therefore, speak of hair-dyes as the only means of service in concealing gray hair.

The means for giving a temporary dark shade to the hair are burnt cork, frankincense black, hard pomatum, and leaden combs. None of these are either neat, durable, or satisfactory in color. For stage purposes, private theatricals, masquerades, and so forth, the hard pomatum is the best.

The dyes are intended to give a natural color which will be reasonably permanent. A great deal of ingenuity has been expended in searching for some chemical preparation which will strike a rich color promptly, without staining the skin, or injuring the hair or the general health. The search has been unsuccessful. No such compound has been found.

We shall not go over the long catalogue of mineral and vegetable materials that are now used for the purpose, but confine ourselves to what we consider from our own observation, which has been extensive enough to justify us in having an opinion on the subject, to be the best.

This is, first, nitrate of silver. This yields, when properly diluted and skilfully applied, rich, natural shades, from a light brown to a jet black. The objections to it are that it stains the skin, that it has been known to be absorbed into the system, and lead to that blueness of the whole surface which we have mentioned, and that if applied too strong, too often, or awkwardly, it will injure the hair. As the stains on the skin can be removed, and the other objections can be avoided by judicious use. they are not serious.

The strength of the solution used for a full black, is a drachm and a half of the nitrate to two ounces of distilled water. To give a rich brown, dilute some of this with an equal amount of distilled water, and for a light brown with double the quantity of water.

This simple solution will, in a few hours after application, yield the desired hue, but it is customary to use a mordant, to "strike the color" at once. The following is one of the best:—

Take—

Of sulphuret of potassium	three drachms ;
Distilled water	two ounces ;
Liquor of potassa	a drachm and a half ;
Oil of anise seed	a few drops.

The hair is first thoroughly cleansed from dust and grease by washing in soap and water, or in water containing a little solution of ammonia. The hair is then allowed to dry, and is next moistened with the mordant, diluted with four or five times its bulk of water. After a few minutes, the nitrate of silver solution is rapidly and thoroughly applied by a fine tooth comb or small brush, the hairs being touched close to their roots, but the skin avoided. This part of the process is delicate, and to do it well requires a skilful hand.

Such an operation, if submitted to once a month,

will yield more satisfactory results than any other for this purpose, provided—and the proviso is all important—that the materials are all of the very best quality, and the " artist" fully equal to the emergency.

Next to nitrate of silver, the walnut dyes are to be placed. They yield various shades of brown, according to their strength, and are quite innocent, but are objectionable on account of staining the skin. They can be prepared in the domestic laboratory by boiling in but little water the hulls of green walnuts (*Juglans nigra*), and straining and bottling the decoction. The hair should be thoroughly cleansed by a wash containing ammonia (very weak, always, as a strong solution is harmful), and the dye applied with a tooth-brush. An elegant dye is prepared by some pharmaceutists from the extract of green walnuts, which can be purchased with full directions for its use.

Vast quantities of sugar of lead have been used of late years for a dye. It is usually compounded with glycerine, water, flowers of sulphur, and some aromatic and coloring substances. This is the composition of nine out of ten of the hair restorers, hair tonics, and hair washes, so loudly advertised all over the country.

No doubt the lead and sulphur do darken the hair, but the color they yield is a dirty brown, not at all natural or pleasing. This is not all. We must condemn this mixture, or any mixture for this purpose containing lead, as dangerous to health and life. Seve-

ral cases have come within our own knowledge within
the last year or two, where lead palsy, lead colic, and
fatal poisoning, were caused by the use of just such
hair-dyes. Very recently a physician of Davenport,
Iowa, who for four years had employed a lead dye for
his hair and beard, perished with all the symptoms of
lead poison. A chemical examination proved that the
metal had been absorbed by the skin, and was present
in his internal organs.

Some persons, it must be remembered, are extremely
susceptible to the influence of the metal. They cannot
employ such a hair-wash for a month without feeling
bad effects. Others again may use it for years with
impunity. The latter have no right to offer their experience as proof that such a mixture is harmless. A
much wider experience than they can possess proves
that it is perilous. We can at this present moment
point to a lady hopelessly paralyzed by lead absorbed
from a hair dye. The extensive and indiscriminate
use of these mixtures deservedly meets with repro-
bation from physicians, while at the same time their
harmlessness in many cases is conceded.

Of late years the ancient fashion has revived, which
sets store by light hair beyond all other. The exact
hue desired approaches that of a silver alloy of gold,
or still more precisely, that of clean, well-cured, bright,
wheaten straw. From the most remote ages, this hue,
no doubt because of its similarity to that of the most

precious of metals, has been held in high esteem. In
Carthage, before Cato had carried into act his oft-
repeated threat, the belles and fops had devised some
art, now lost, to change their natural black locks to
a golden yellow.

Rome under the empire was seized with the same
mania. When dyeing did not suffice, quite a trade
was started with the fair-haired German tribes beyond
the Alps, who sold their locks to Latin merchants, to
be worn on the heads of Roman dandies. All through
the Middle Ages, we discover proofs of the same taste.

The Spanish and Italian ladies of the fifteenth century dampened their black tresses with muriatic acid,
and sate in the sun to bleach it to the coveted yellow.
Therefore Don Quixote describes his Dulcinea as having " hair the color of gold," and Dante commences
one of his *Canzone* with the line—

> " Io miro i crespi e gli biondi capegli."

Shakspeare in his Sonnets tells us such was the value
of yellow hair in his day, that even that of the dead
was cut off and sold :—

> " Before the golden tresses of the dead,
>   The right of sepulchres, were shorn away,
>   To live a second life on second head ;
>   Ere beauty's dead fleece made another gay," etc.

At times, fine gold thread was worn in place of hair.
Thus, history informs us that when Charles the Bold,

Duke of Burgundy, had met his death in battle with
the Swiss, his body was taken from the ditch where it
was found, and interred with princely pomp. On his
face he wore instead of the natural growth, a long
beard of golden thread.

The ancient method of producing this color artificially is lost, but a score of others have risen in its
place. Those that produce the best effect are likewise
the most critical to use, and are probably injurious.
We have before us the analyses of four of the most
popular " golden-hair fluids," " warranted to impart a
rich, golden, flaxen shade, to hair of any color after a
few applications." They are all alike, and are all but
modern adaptations of the plan of the Spanish damsels
three hundred years ago, which we have mentioned
above. The active ingredient in all of them is muriatic acid, which they contain in about the proportion
of twenty drops of the " officinal" dilute nitro-muriatic
acid to the ounce of distilled water. Coloring matter
and aromatic substances make up the remainder of
these magic preparations. No doubt they would effect
the purpose for which they are intended, but whether
they would do so without hurting the skin or hair is
less certain.

The acid thus weakened does not irritate an ordinary
skin, it is true, but doubtless would one which was
delicate. We have not had the opportunity to ascertain whether they cause falling of the hair. Those

willing to take the risk can use them, as no bad results
to the general health follow the external application of
a weak solution of this acid.   On the contrary, it is a
useful addition to a bath for "bilious" persons.

If persons *will* use a golden dye, this is the one we
recommend.   Many of the others contain a salt of
mercury (the yellow sulphuret), or one of lead (the
acetate, nitrate, or yellow chromate), or of antimony
(the yellow sulphuret), all of which are poisonous and
objectionable.

ON FALSE HAIR, CHIGNONS, ETC.

The most crabbed moralist, we presume, will hardly
object to false hair in the shape of a wig—but when it
comes to a "chignon," or a "rat," or a "curl," the
offence is singularly apparent.   We confess to a want
of power to see this difference, and believe that if it is
proper in the one instance to improve the looks by the
use of borrowed locks, so it is in the other.   Women
are quite right to wear what amount of false hair they
need to dress their heads becomingly.

The trade in human hair is a very important branch
of commerce.   It has increased more than fourfold
within the last twelve years, and yet the demand so far
exceeds the supply that the prices have also increased
fourfold.   In Philadelphia, where we write, a good-
sized braid of very choice hair, weighing about sixteen

ounces, costs from five to ten dollars the ounce, as we learn from dealers.

These may seem exorbitant figures, but if we compare them with the prices in former generations, we find they are not at all unparalleled. A story is told in the Percy Anecdotes of the Countess of Suffolk, in the reign of George I. She was visiting with her husband the Court of Hanover, and, as is not unfrequent with travellers, they ran out of money at some town where they had no acquaintances. The Countess had, however, magnificent hair, and as she was a shifty woman, she sent for the most fashionable friseur, and sold it to him for the amount of twenty pounds sterling, a sum equal in value to a hundred and fifty dollars in gold to-day.

We have found even higher figures than this, much higher, obtained for fine hair. One instance is recorded of about the same date, where one hundred pounds sterling was paid for an uncommonly fine head. This eclipses any price we have heard quoted in our day.

The chief cause why some colors are so much dearer than others, is the great difficulty of dyeing the hair after it is cut. It is next to impossible to persuade it to take the bright, delicate, glossy hues most admired.

A century ago the hair trade depended chiefly on wig-making. It was *de rigueur* that every gentleman should wear an immense wig when in full dress. On one occasion Lord Bolingbroke was sent for in haste by Queen Anne about some pressing public business. Aware of its importance, he hurried to her presence without taking time to change his wig, which was a "tie," and not a "full-bottomed" one, as he should have worn on entering such august presence. The Queen noticed the neglect, and after he was gone, pettishly exclaimed:—

"I suppose his lordship will come next time in his night-cap."

The trade of the *perruquier* in those days was by odds the most important of the cosmetic callings. These old-fashioned wigs are still retained in England by judges on the bench, and, singularly enough, by the liveried footmen of the wealthy. No one else dreams of wearing them.

The demand for hair now comes chiefly from the ladies, and the commodity is made up not so much in the shape of wigs, toupées, etc., as into braids, curls, chignons, etc. The London trade-reports, however, showed that during our civil war a brisk business was carried on in false whiskers and moustaches. It commenced at the beginning and dropped off at the end of our war. It puzzled the Londoners to account for this sudden and large demand, as well as for its equally sudden cessation when our armies were disbanded.

As, in following our destiny, it so happened that during most of the war we held a position in the army which let us into divers secrets of the service, the solution of the puzzle was easy enough to us. There were, in the first place, thousands of spies, secret agents, and fugitives, both men and women, who resorted to these artifices for disguise. Secondly, and here the bulk of the trade was, very many officers, especially in cities, were accustomed to be absent without leave, and to frequent places where they did not wish to be recognized by their superiors, or by the enlisted men of their commands. Hence, they kept by them a citizen's dress and these disguises, for use on such escapades. This we know was a very general habit.

A few years ago an absurd clamor was raised by some sensational papers about the alleged discovery of minute ova—nits, in plain terms—on the hair sold for chignons. It was asserted that any one who wore them exposed her head to the invasion of very unwelcome guests of the insect kind. Small masses called gregarines were pointed out on some hair as these pretended ova. There was not a word of scientific truth in all this. The methods employed to prepare hair for market will certainly clean it thoroughly from all such impurities, and the gregarines, when examined by competent microscopists, turn out to be nothing but very minute fungi, entirely harmless to the skin, and also very rarely met with on false hair of any kind.

25

FALLING OF THE HAIR, AND BALDNESS.

Hitherto we have spoken of the hair in health. We shall now review its most common diseases, and give their home treatment.

The scalp is subject to most of the affections which attack other portions of the skin, and also to some which are peculiar to itself. Some of them are unusually obstinate, and most of them are less easily treated on account of the covering of hair and the feeble circulation on the top of the head.

More common than any single one of these diseases is a gradual falling or thinning of the hair, without visible cause. It occurs usually between the ages of twenty and thirty, and in women more frequently than in men. Sometimes it commences during pregnancy, or in the late summer. The hair is reproduced very slowly, and has a dry, withered look, the partings become more and more visible, and finally there is an unmistakable tendency to a bald spot on the crown.

Such a state of things causes well-founded alarm, and one " hair-restorer" after another, mentioned in the newspapers and on bill-posters, is tried, and tried in vain. The young lady becomes distressed at the prospect of baldness. and is ready to take advantage of any means that will restore the glossy locks of yore. Let us see what we can do to assist her.

This thinning of the hair arises from some definite

cause—be sure of that; and be sure that if the cause is removed the hair will regain its vigor. The cause may lie in the condition of the scalp itself, or, so intimate is the sympathy of all parts of this body of ours, it may depend upon the disturbed action of some remote internal organ.

It may seem strange to say that dyspepsia is a frequent cause of loss of hair—yet this is undoubtedly true, and no tonics or restorers will do a particle of good until the dyspepsia is cured. Complaints peculiar to the sex are another fertile cause. and general debility brought about by watching, overwork. bad air, or irregular habits, is likewise often to blame. These general disorders must be remedied by a timely course of medicine, the blood must be purified, the secretions regulated, the skin brought into healthy action, and then we can with great confidence go to work on the head itself.

If the scalp is very carefully examined with a lens, it will usually be found in such cases not so healthy as it looks at first sight. There will appear some dryness, or scurfiness, or irritability; the roots of the hairs will be found reddened and spongy; the surface will feel hot; some odor other than natural will be perceived. It may be that while all seems sound to the naked eye, the microscope will at once reveal a wide-spread local disease.

Supposing the scurfiness to be slight, and no eruption present, the treatment must be commenced by a gentle wash in tepid water with Castile or sulphur soap. No harsh soap must be used, and secret or rancid applications must be avoided. The head once cleaned, it should for a fortnight be oiled night and morning with a small quantity of the following mixture, which should be brushed into the skin with a soft tooth-brush :—

Take—

| Of pure glycerine | three drachms ; |
| Lime-water | four ounces. |

This will bring the skin into a more healthy condition, and prepare it for the advantageous use of a stimulating wash, which it is not well to employ at the outset. There are hundreds of these washes or hair tonics advertised, very few of which deserve any praise. The prices charged for them are high, the materials are often dangerous, and of inferior quality. In place of them, we shall give several receipts for approved tonics which we have used in our own practice with satisfaction, and which can be obtained from any apothecary.

After two weeks the above mentioned formula can be used with the addition of half an ounce of tincture of cantharides, and later with one ounce of the tincture. The brushing should be more persistent, enough to bring a slight redness to the surface. Or the following lotion may be employed :—

Take—

Of castor oil	one ounce ;
Liquor of ammonia (strong)	one ounce ;
Best French brandy	two ounces ;
Rose water	six ounces.

This should not be used more frequently than every other day.   The following may be applied morning and evening :—

Strong decoction of Peruvian bark	half a pint ;
Brandy	wineglassful
Glycerine	tablespoonful.

We have also seen the following " home recipe" do good service :—

Old whiskey	half a pint ;
Rock salt	as much as will dissolve ;
Glycerine	a tablespoonful
Flour of sulphur	a teaspoonful.

The Rev. John Wesley used to recommend in threatened baldness to rub the scalp with the freshly-cut surface of a raw onion.   As this is quite an active stimulant, the advice is unquestionably sound, though the application is certainly not elegant.   Water in which mustard has been boiled, the juice of horseradish, the spirits of garden thyme and rosemary, and many similar articles have local popularity as hair tonics.   They all depend for their virtues on the power they have to stimulate the scalp.   Probably the lotions we have given above are better than any of them.

A very effectual stimulant, and one we especially recommend on account of the ease and neatness with which ladies with long hair can have it applied, and the excellent effects it has, is electricity, or its modification, galvanism. A current of moderate force should be passed through the scalp for fifteen or twenty minutes daily. This excites the action of the blood-vessels, and restores the nervous force to the part. It may be regarded, when judiciously and regularly applied, as at once the most efficient and the neatest hair tonic known, where local debility is the trouble. Nor does its use interfere with the other means which we have suggested.

Finally, shaving the head may be resorted to. This, as we have previously said, is not approved by many, and there are no doubt numerous cases where it would be ill advised. Nor can it be expected to have marked results, unless other means are also employed. The shaving should be performed once a week for at least three months, in order to obtain its full effect, and in the meantime the scalp should be stimulated daily by electricity, the cold bath, frictions with strong liniments, or brushing. When all these are attended to, as well as the general health, there is a very good chance that one or the other will prove efficacious, and the hair be materially strengthened.

Even when baldness has actually appeared, the case is not always desperate. If the victim has patience, she may recover a very respectable share of hair by the diligent employment of the same means. Some physicians commence by blistering the bald scalp, so as to restore it to a more vigorous life, and the result often proves the wisdom of the proceeding. The same end may be attained by vigorous inunction of tincture of cantharides, or oil of cajuput, which latter has a high reputation as a trichogēne.

That variety of baldness which appears in entirely bare spots over the head, while the hair around them is as thick as ever (*alopecia areata*), may often be healed with great promptness by rubbing thoroughly into the spots every morning and evening a little oil of turpentine. The bareness should cease extending after a few days, and after a few weeks small downy hairs should be perceptible, rising on the white skin. This is one of those venerable remedies which we find mentioned in writers as far back as the Roman empire, and which every few years some person, in ignorance of its antiquity, discovers anew, and makes loud laudations of it. But this only goes to show that it is really a trusty application.

DANDRIFF, AND SCURF OF THE SCALP.

When one brushes and combs the most healthy hair which has been neglected for a few days. more or less fine whitish scales will be brushed out, such as we are very apt to see on the coat-collars of gentlemen too busy or too careless to dust their clothes. This is called dandriff, and is simply the scarf-skin which has served its time, and has been thrown off, as it constantly is from every part of the body. Its presence in moderate quantities signifies nothing, except as an admonition to greater cleanliness.

When, however, this branny dust becomes quite conspicuous in amount, it betokens some disease of the skin. A close examination may reveal several reddish patches over the head, with irregular but well-defined outlines surrounded with a red margin, which patches are covered with minute white scales, and have a slightly itchy feeling. The hair upon them is thin and weakened, showing dry and flattened under the microscope, if they have been of long standing. This is the complaint called in medical works *pityriasis capitis.* It is very common, and is a fertile cause of loss of the hair.

If it is taken early, the following ointment well rubbed on the spots every morning, after the skin has been carefully cleaned by soap and water, will effect a speedy cure :—

Powdered borax	a scruple;
Dilute solution of subacetate of lead	two drachms;
Clean lard	one ounce;
Otto of roses, or any scent	a few drops.

Or the first two ingredients may be dissolved in three ounces of rain-water, and half an ounce of glycerine.

In old and obstinate cases, some internal medicine may be necessary, but often the above, or the use of the wash containing spirits of ammonia, given in the last section, will answer. The diet must be looked to. It should be plain, but sufficient, without coffee, liquors, or anything heating, and half a bottle or a bottle of citrate of magnesia should be taken once or twice a week according to circumstances. By these means, continued for some time after the red patches have disappeared, persons will rarely fail in curing themselves.

At other times, close inspection will show that the scales of dandriff proceed from minute vesicles which rise on the skin, break, and dry up. They are very apt to escape attention altogether, unless they are searched for. This is a condition of *eczema*, as it is called, and will be sure to be followed by the loss of the hair in time.

Or again, a common aspect of neglected hair is one presenting little patches on which a yellowish mass of scales are collected, not dry and branny, but oily, or hardened into crusts.

Both these conditions must be referred to the family physician, as they require too active medicines for home treatment.

This is also the case with those common complaints of children, "scalled head," and "ring-worm." both of which lead to destruction of the hair and baldness.

Whenever there seems a tendency to any disease of the kind we have described, it is well to use in washing the head—which should be done twice a week—a soap medicated with juniper tar or carbolic acid. These soaps can be obtained from most apothecaries. It is *not* well to comb or brush violently the hair, when there is such an inflammatory condition present. First let the disease be cured, and the skin resume its healthy action, before it is stimulated. For the same reason it is a serious blunder which many commit, to apply at once hair tonics or pomades containing stimulating substances to their scalps already in a state of irritation. On the contrary, cooling lotions or soothing ointments are required until the irritation is removed, and then the circulation and innervation of the parts should be encouraged, if they require it. Frequently, without any such means being called in, the hair, as soon as freed from the disease, against which it has been battling, will at once commence to grow thick and strong.

EXCESSIVE GROWTH OF HAIR, AND DEPILATORIES.

There is such a thing as having too much hair, as well as too little, and the tendency is particularly destructive to beauty, when it displays itself on uncovered portions of the body, where hair ought not to grow. Not unfrequently the front hair encroaches on the forehead, injuring its outlines and imprinting a coarse expression on the features. The neck may be over-grown by a short unmanageable growth. The eyebrows are occasionally connected by scattered bristles. In brunettes, especially, there is liability to the appearance of a delicate moustache on the upper lip, and a development of coarseish dark hair on the forearms. After a certain age, particularly in single women, both chin and upper lip are apt to be invaded by a short beard, not at all attractive. Moles and birth-marks are usually planted with a hairy growth, and in the nostrils and the ears a bristly tuft is often found. All these are incompatible with good looks, and in the interest of beauty should be removed.

We might add some curious examples of " bearded women." They are by no means rare, and hardly a season passes by, that one or more are not exhibited by some travelling showman. The cause of their peculiarity seems to lie in an over-excited condition of the hair bulbs, which usually commences in youth. Julia Pastrana was a Spanish opera dancer of some celebrity, who a few years ago visited England and, we believe, this country also. She had a fine silken beard about four inches in length, and was unusually hairy over the whole of her body. Still more curious, she had with her a little daughter, but a few years old, whose body already showed signs of the Esau-like hairiness which characterized her mother.

Some diseases are accompanied or followed by an

extraordinary growth of hair, not only on the head, but over the whole body. This is occasionally observable in consumptives, after violent fevers, and in the course of diseases peculiar to the sex. The fact offers us another opportunity for remarking, that the consideration of the hair and its diseases can never be separated from the study of the physiology and maladies of the whole body.

The Oriental ladies have a horror of superfluous hairs, and destroy them with the most sedulous care. Therefore the cosmetic science of Western Europe, which was a creation of later date, first learned the secret of depilatories, or hair-removing compounds, from their Eastern neighbors.

The preparation chiefly used in the Asiatic harems is called the *rusma*. For a long time its composition was unknown, but now-a-days it is not easy to conceal the ingredients of a mixture from the prying eyes of the chemist. The true Oriental rusma has been carefully analyzed, and found to be composed of a form of arsenic, called arsenical iron pyrites, and quicklime, in the proportion of two parts of the former to one part of the latter, both in fine powder.

It is imitated by mixing one part of the yellow sulphuret of arsenic, known in commerce as orpiment, with quicklime, and powdered starch. This is made into a paste with water, and laid on the part from which it is intended to remove the hair. As soon as much smarting is felt, the paste is removed by washing with tepid water, and the hairs will come away with it. Unless this is done skilfully, however, an ugly scar may be left, or the system poisoned by the arsenic. We therefore warn our readers against using this or any depilatory, of which they do not know the composition, as most of the latter, whether they deny it or not, contain some arsenical salt. We shall give some more innocent and quite efficient formulæ, which will answer as well or better than the imitation of rusma.

The safest of all chemical depilatories is what is called the sulphydrate of calcium —

Take—

| Of sulphuret of calcium | two parts ; |
| Quicklime | one part. |

Powder them separately, mix, and keep in a well-stopped bottle. When wanted for use, make into a paste with a little water, and spread on the part. Let it remain for fifteen minutes, or until it smarts, and then wash off with soap and tepid water.

Another equally safe, recommended by the distinguished French surgeon Cazenave, is :—

Quicklime	one part ;
Carbonate of soda	two parts ;
Lard	eight parts.

Mix to form an ointment.

These do not answer in every case, and the former

26

on sensitive skins may leave an unpleasant though temporary redness.

Professor Redwood some years since lauded in very high terms a strong solution of the sulphuret of barium as a depilatory. When used, it must be mixed rapidly with finely-powdered starch, and applied to the part. Its application demands skill and care, and with these, it is a very good depilatory.

But all the barium salts are poisonous, and though this is undoubtedly an efficient preparation, as there are other and innocuous means, we advise them to be patronized in place of others.

In preference to any of these chemical depilatories we prefer the mechanical. This is simply pulling the hairs out " by the roots." This has an alarming sound, and suggests torture. But there is no occasion for terror. If properly performed, the operation is painless. Fine tweezers, or " ciliary forceps," may be used, and the sensation of the part previously blunted by pressing against it firmly a piece of ice, or allowing the spray of ether to fall upon it for a few seconds.

An old-fashioned method for heroic beauties used to be to press firmly upon the part a piece of shoemaker's wax, in which the hairs would become firmly imbedded, and then jerk it away, hairs and all! This demands an amount of heroism to which modern belles are rarely equal, and modern chemistry, therefore. ever obedient to the demands of its queens, has contrived a composition which is destined, we think, to supersede most other depilatories on account of the ease with which it is applied, its painlessness, and its satisfactory results.

It is resin tempered with wax, with the addition of a strong anodyne. The mixture is melted and run into sticks, like sealing wax. The end of one of these sticks is softened and warmed by bringing it near a candle, but is not allowed to become hot enough to burn the skin, and is pressed firmly on the hairy spot for about a minute. It is then suddenly pulled away, bringing the hair with it, and this *without any pain.* The only skill required is to heat the end of the stick to the proper point, so that it will hold firmly the hairs, and not scorch the skin.

As this *psilothron*, as it is called, is at present not manufactured in this country, so far as we know, we have called the attention of some of the dealers in toilet articles to it, so that it can now be obtained through several merchants in this and other cities.

We do not advise using it, or any other depilatory, for the hairs in the nostrils or in the ears. These are very sensitive parts of our body, in the vicinity of delicate and important organs, which it is not well to imperil in the least. A thin-bladed and blunt-pointed pair of scissors should be used to clip the growth in these spots from time to time, but only when they are unusually coarse. For these are the natural veils and

dust-catchers, which wise Nature has hung at the entrance to these cavities.

THE ARRANGEMENT OF THE HAIR.

"The arrangement of the hair! Why, that is matter for a barber, or a dressing-maid. We leave it to
them, and to the fashion-plate makers."

The worse for you if you do, for it is simply throwing away one of the most potent means of enhancing
the natural charms. The ancients, passionate lovers
of beauty, with souls ever sensitive of its sweet con-
cords, did not so. They thought it no derogation to
bestow on the disposition of the locks thought and
study. Neither do we.

The symbol-loving minds of the Greeks saw in the
various modes of wearing the hair the expression of
different temperaments, and ever strove to adopt that
which was at once in the most perfect harmony with
the features, and with the character of the individuals.
Let us try to obtain, if we can, some small share of
their artistic power, some partial insight into that wondrous world of beauty which they saw surrounding the
daily life of this work-a-day world, where we, alas, see
little but hard facts and homely fancies. How much
will be our gain if we learn to see the beautiful, not
only in galleries of statuary and paintings, but in the
forms of daily life!

Perhaps, after all, we have more of this insight than

one might at first think. Some one asked the sculptor
Phidias, whence he drew the inspiration which guided
him in his statue of the Olympian Jupiter. He replied, "In the verses of Homer." And we do not fail
to recognize in the masses of locks which crown the
head of that wondrous work, the hair, which, in the
Homeric poems, shakes, by its movement, Olympus itself. So Christian art, recognizing the subtle harmony
which exists between the disposition of the hair and
the character, ever portrays the meek and lowly Mes-
siah with blonde or light brown hair, resting in tranquil
waves over a forehead whereon reign a celestial serenity
and a more than human benignity, and falling upon
the drooping shoulders which bore the bitter Cross of
Calvary. Can any point in these two conceptions of
divinity bring more clearly to the appreciative mind
the difference between the heathen and the Christian
faith?

Ancient art in all its creations looked to this element
of the beautiful. The Furies, Medea, Gorgon, are
portrayed with wild and dishevelled locks, but the
queenly Venus of Milo, and the Venus de Medici, have
abundant, slightly curly, gently waving hair, suited
to the repose of perfect beauty.

Such facts as these, if well considered, point to a
theory of hair-dressing which as yet the *friseurs* know
nothing about, and the ladies of the great world are
far from appreciating. But do not think that we have

any idea of advancing and explaining this theory. Far from it. We have already disclaimed any intention to be reformers. It is not a trade to our taste. Nevertheless, in a gentle and modest way, we would like to offer a few hints on this matter, and won't feel in the least offended if they are passed over with quiet nonchalance, for that is a fate we expect for them.

These are to the effect that in the selection of a *frisure*, as in that of colors, a lady should take into account her complexion, her stature, her features, and her expression, and so arrange the hair as to heighten and give greater prominence to the most favorable parts of these, and conceal or diminish any defect which they may present. Precisely in the same manner as two clever artists have spoken of the law of hues when adapted to dress,[1] so would we speak of the hair. If we are asked to apply these principles, and state exactly which modes of arrangement are most becoming, we hesitate to do so, partly, perhaps, out of diffidence, partly because we do not think it quite germain to our present theme. We shall not hesitate, however, to express in general terms what in the interest of a sound hygiene should be the characteristics of *every* coiffure. It should exert no violence on the hairs, but

[1] Color in Dress: A Manual for Ladies. By W. & G. Audsley. This valuable little book merits a careful study by every woman who would dress to the best advantage.

allow them to lay as much as possible in their natural
folds; it should not twist the hairs tightly, nor separate them in a great many bands, but fold them loosely,
and allow them to be well aired; it should not keep the
hairs in one position, especially if that be an unnatural
one, for any great length of time; it should never impart to the features an ignoble or fatuous expression;
it should not imitate one of the lower varieties of our
race, and still less should it resemble the disposition of
the hair on any of the inferior animals; it should aim at
simplicity, not require much network or artifices to
keep it in position, not heat the head, nor strain the
hairs, nor be of much weight; it should neither oblige
the wearer to expose the half-protected or quite uncovered scalp to the sun and blasts, nor yet by its
thickness prevent the ventilation and unobstructed
passage of secretions necessary to the health of the
hair-bulb. In short, as the English balladist sings :—

> " Hair loosely flowing, robes as free,
>   Such sweet neglect more pleaseth me,
>   Than all the trickeries of art
>   Which strike the eye, but not the heart."

There is nothing new in these views. " The characteristics of beautiful hair," says a distinguished writer
on the subject, "have ever been what they are now.
The simple natural arrangement of the hair has the
same charms for us that the ancients conceded it.
None but the artists of the Middle Ages could perceive

any beauty in stiff and formal styles, and with them it was owing to an ascetic exaltation which led them to quench in feminine beauty everything which pertained to passion and the senses, and to portray their seraphic ideals without a soft curve or a graceful touch to relieve their sainted immobility."

We may add some advice about the propriety—in an artistic sense—of making use of coloring matters for the hair when gray, and on the employment of false hair and wigs. The story is related of the Emperor Augustus, that on one occasion he found his daughter Julia undergoing the operation of having her gray hairs plucked from her head by her tire-woman. " Would you prefer, my daughter," said the Emperor, " to be gray, or to be bald?" She replied that grayness was more to her mind. " Then," rejoined her father, " why do you adopt the most certain means to be bald?" The Emperor's question has a wider application, for many a one, eagerly recurring to some of the advertised means of darkening the hair, have learned only too late that thereby they have exchanged grayness for baldness.

There are some faces which are decidedly improved by gray hair. They acquire a dignity and attractiveness, which they never previously had. Like some landscapes, their charms are greatest when covered with the snows of the winter time of life. Such faces should never be marred by dyed hair.

It is contrary to all good taste to have the hair display the raven hue of youth when the marks of age are conspicuous on the face and the figure. For this reason, if it is decided to wear a wig, one should be chosen which suits with the whole appearance, and not simply with the desire to give to the top of the head an air of juvenility which is flatly contradicted by all other parts of the person.

Wigs, to speak of them a little more at length, should be as light as possible, readily permeable to the exterior air, so that the functions of the skin are not interfered with. They should not be too firmly fastened to the scalp, and they should be removed as frequently as possible, lest their warmth or weight lead to some eruption or other disease of the skin beneath. There is no call for their use merely for grayness, and when they are worn merely for the sake of allowing the hairs to gain strength by repeated shaving, the precautions we have mentioned, most of which have been already urged by Professor Cazenave in his excellent treatise on the hair, should be redoubled.